Freaky
FLORIDA

Freaky FLORIDA

THE WONDERHOUSE, THE DEVIL'S TREE, THE SHAMAN OF PHILIPPE PARK AND MORE

Mark Muncy and Kari Schultz

THE
History
PRESS

Published by The History Press
Charleston, SC
www.historypress.com

Copyright © 2018 by Mark Muncy and Kari Schultz
All rights reserved

Cover illustrations by Kari Schultz.

Opposite: Map of Florida pointing out various tourist attractions. 1938. *State Archives of Florida, Florida Memory.*

First published 2018

Manufactured in the United States

ISBN 9781467140355

Library of Congress Control Number: 2018942440

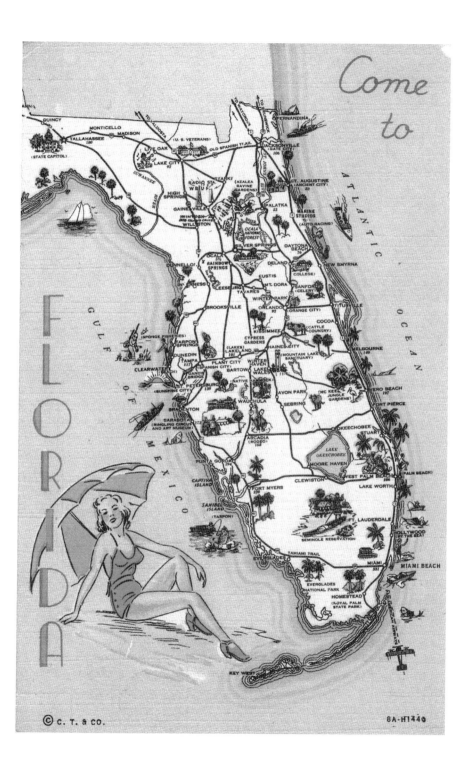

CONTENTS

CONTENTS

ACKNOWLEDGEMENTS

Kari and I know that no book comes out of just the work of the author and illustrator. This book is no different. We must thank our friends and families for their continued support. You all have our eternal gratitude.

A very special thank-you, as always, goes to Marta Jones, archivist at the St. Petersburg Museum of History. We could not have completed the book without your amazing skills and ability to find even the most obscure reference for us. The museum itself is a gem and gets a full chapter within.

Elizabeth Abbott helped us in so many ways and is an amazing friend. Between pre-editing, being a travel companion and working as convention support staff, we couldn't have made it through either book without you.

My daughters, Callie and Beth Muncy, acted as backup drivers on several trips. They long suffered growing up with a haunted house in our backyard. The fact that they still talk to me is incredible. The fact that they still go on crazy adventures with their old man is just wild.

We also have to thank our volunteer editors for this book. The brilliant authors Amanda Byrd and Allison Williams stepped up to bat for us. The incomparable Vanya Glyr also lent her amazing linguistic skills to the task of editing early on. We owe you a red-ink cartridge badly. Dani Cervantes, Susan Irving and Megan Rogers lent even more eyes on the initial edits.

Dale Aden Jr. played backup driver on one trip. Having been the beating heart of Hellview Cemetery for so long, it was nice to hit the open road with an old friend for a drive deep into the heart of Nowhere, Florida.

Contributors, interview subjects and other special people of note include Doug Stenroos, Owl Goingback, Jim Stafford, Sally Gage, Jennifer Sunday and David Sidotti. Special thanks go out to each and every one of you for helping so much.

Once again, we thank Nancy Alloy at Books at Park Place and the crew at Trader Joe's in St. Petersburg for covering us for all those trips and events we keep having to go to. Thanks for putting up with us and letting us keep our jobs another year.

Finally, we have to thank the wonderful folks at Arcadia Publishing and The History Press for these last few years of support. Amanda, Jonny, Joe, Ryan, Crystal and Katie, you are all simply amazing and the best help we could have ever asked for.

INTRODUCTION

For those of you who read our last book, *Eerie Florida: Chilling Tales from the Panhandle to the Keys*, which came out in September 2017, I'd like to say, "Welcome back." For those of you who haven't read it yet, you can go pick it up and we'll wait right here for you. If you can't get hold of it, can't wait or aren't a fan of eerie things, then let us give you a quick rundown of who we are. The rest of you can skip ahead four paragraphs.

For those of you just joining us, here are the basics. We ran a haunted house for twenty years in St. Petersburg, Florida, called Hellview Cemetery. It was named after a local lost Tampa Bay cemetery called Hillview. We based the entire haunted attraction on local lore and legends collected throughout the Sunshine State. We creatively embellished the legends for the haunted house crowds as was needed to scare our audience. As the attraction gained in popularity, so did the legends.

We collected the stories on our website and eventually in a book called *31 Tales of Hellview Cemetery* from Purple Cart Publishing. One year later, we were asked to remove the stuff we completely fabricated and re-release it with all new stories as *Tales of Terror of Tampa Bay*. Both books sold well at the haunt and in local bookstores.

We were constantly asked about the original non-embellished versions of the legends. We had assumed that the stories were common knowledge, as we had known them well. Some of our tales were gaining fame through the popularity of the "Creepypasta" phenomena (a Wikipedia-like page for urban legends) that was sweeping the Internet at the time. Several of our stories had been copied and pasted right into Creepypasta website and popular Reddit forums. We had no idea of the fame of our own mythology. Once word got back to us, we decided that it was time to remind people of the original legends.

In late 2016, we watched the last remnants of what had been St. Petersburg's infamous Hellview Cemetery be carted away by garbage trucks. Twenty years of a historic charity haunted house were fading back into nothingness and legend, a victim of our own popularity. We began to work on *Eerie Florida* for The History Press soon after. That book was a collection of the monsters, myths and legends from the dark side of Florida history.

We traveled more than three thousand miles and never left the state. We visited everywhere from the Gulf Breeze UFO flap in the panhandle to Robert the Haunted Doll down in Key West. As we traveled and toured, people would tell us about even more legends, ghost stories and crazy places. We knew there was going to be at least one more book filled with just as much history as *Eerie Florida*.

The book came out in September 2017, one year after Hellview Cemetery closed its doors (for now). We toured many conventions and bookstores throughout the state. We were on numerous podcasts and radio and TV shows. E-mails started choking out our mail servers at EerieFlorida.com with more and more stories for us to investigate. We were already compiling notes for the inevitable second book, but we wanted to do more than just retread old ground.

A few locations we had visited had no place in *Eerie Florida*. Some of these had no supernatural or paranormal ties. Many we simply wanted to write about were just odd, quirky or plain fun. Other locations we couldn't include in the previous book needed more research than we had time for during our quickly looming deadline.

We hit the road once again to collect the photos we would need for this second book while touring for the last one. This time around, we also sought out more historical societies, museums and new interviews. We quickly realized that places like Solomon's Castle and the Wonderhouse needed to find a home in the new volume thanks to meeting the wonderful families involved with each of these places. Our working title with The History Press became "Strange Florida." It would still include ghosts, monsters and legends, but this time, we could include some incredible places just for fun as well.

So, here we are. We've traveled another 3,500 miles, and we still haven't managed to cross the border into Georgia, Mississippi, Louisiana or

Alabama. At every stop, we explored more and more lore and ghost stories. Along the way, we discovered some other incredible hidden gems and are glad to share them here. We even got to put on our "Indiana Jones" gear and head out on a real expedition into the heart of a few swamps with fresh leads on old legends.

I'd like to say that we've reached the end, but every rock we overturn seems to give us even more stories to tell. Some people have told us new versions of tales we covered previously. Some new witnesses have stepped forward after our first publication to add more details to the legends we uncovered. I'm certain that more will come out after the publication of this book as well. We've been updating EerieFlorida.com with new information as we receive it.

The book is laid out like a travel guide from mostly north to south, with some zigzags across the state. If you decided to use this or *Eerie Florida* for some legend-tripping of your own, please be sure to be respectful of private property. Please take only pictures and leave only footprints at these sites, many of which are natural habitats. Pay proper respect to the many victims of tragedies and oppression we sadly have to discuss to give historical context. Please do support the local historical societies, national parks and support organizations that help keep so many of these places open to the public. Many are in the process of being restored so that they can eventually be opened to the public. If you are able, donate time or money to these worthy causes.

Here we are once again, dear readers. I feel it only necessary to give the following words of warning before you continue further. We hope that the stories and history you find within these pages thrill you. The tales might shock you. Some might even horrify you. So, if you feel you have a delicate disposition…well, don't say we didn't warn you.

MARK MUNCY
March 3, 2018,
Florida's 173rd birthday

GERONIMO AND FORT PICKENS, PENSACOLA

Fort Pickens, near Pensacola on Santa Rosa Island, is a walled fort steeped in history. The need for coastal forts in the United States goes back to the last time a foreign naval power attacked our lands: the British. The attacks came during the War of 1812. The British Royal Navy sailed right up to the American coast and destroyed the new capital in Washington, D.C. They then sacked several other port cities.

The British were repelled only in Baltimore, thanks primarily to a big brick fort there. The U.S. Congress then passed a law to build forts to guard every major harbor and port along the American eastern coastline, all the way down to Georgia. Florida was still under Spanish control at that time, so it was not included in the initial wave of construction.

In 1817, America purchased Florida from the Spanish for about $5 million. It was brought into the fledgling United States with the Adams-Onis Treaty. To assist in patrolling the coastline of the new state, Congress commissioned the construction of a huge naval yard near what is now Pensacola. They then built three brick forts to protect the harbor, as they had been doing for every major port since the War of 1812. Fort Pickens was the largest of the three fortifications and stood watch over the bay waters for many years.

No foreign power ever attacked the United States' ports again. Some taxpayers said that the forts were a waste of money. Others said that the construction of the forts is what kept the naval base and other ports safe. They believed that all the foreign powers knew that an attack would prove futile. Either way, the deterrent factor of the forts appears to have worked, even if it seemed unnecessary in retrospect.

In January 1861, a young lieutenant received orders at a small fort across Pensacola Bay that had been built on an old Spanish camp. This redoubt was called Fort Barrancas. Lieutenant Adam J. Slemmer was given word that Florida had seceded from the Union and that he was to hold all the forts for the Union. With only fifty soldiers under his command and maybe an additional thirty sailors on loyal boats in the nearby naval yard, the young officer knew that he would be hard-pressed to hold all the forts in the area. He pulled all his forces to Fort Pickens, which lay across the water of the bay, as the most defensible position.

Confederate troops did invade and did indeed take all the other forts, including Fort Barrancas. They also took control of the naval yard. Then the Confederates turned their sights on Fort Pickens. They came three times to demand the surrender of Fort Pickens, but Slemmer and his forces refused to yield the fort. Colonel William Henry Chase of the Florida militia came out to demand the surrender of the fort on the third attempt. Chase had been one of the original architects of the fort. Slemmer again refused.

Colonel Chase told Slemmer that he knew Fort Pickens better than anyone since he had helped design it. Slemmer replied that he and his men had made many changes. If the Confederates wanted the fort, they would have to come and take it. In truth, the only changes Slemmer had made was to turn the cannons toward the other forts and away from the sea. Chase and the Confederates left and prepared to assault.

By the time the Confederates attempted their assault, reinforcements had arrived for the Union. Fort Pickens remained one of the several forts in the South to never fall to the Confederacy throughout the Civil War.

With the fall of the Confederacy and the restoration of the Union, the American government turned the focus of its military might to the West, marching on Native American tribes. Many were forced to give up their lands and move to reservations.

In 1875, the lands of the Apache were situated in what would become Arizona, along the Mexican border. The tribe had already been restricted to 7,200 square miles of territory by forced agreements with the United States government. By the 1880s, that number had been reduced to 2,600 square miles. Tribes who were hostile to each other were being forced closer together and fighting spread. American Indian peoples were already distrustful of the American government, and the Apaches fought against this oppression fiercely.

The settlers in the new Arizona territory were fearful of the Indians. They began to request federal troops to assist them in stopping raiding bands of Apache that had attacked their settlements. As the U.S. Army marched west, the inevitable clashes would forever be a dark spot in American history.

One of these Apache raiding bands soon became notorious. It had gained notoriety for its ability to strike and easily fade away across the border back into Mexico. No one seemed to be able to track the band. It was as if this raiding party was made up of ghosts. This band was led by one they called Geronimo.

Born in 1829 in what is now western New Mexico, Geronimo was a member of the Bedonkohe Apaches. He married into the Chiricahua tribe. Sometime in 1858, this medicine man had to defend his life and that of his family when soldiers from Mexico came to his village and began to slaughter his tribe. With the death of his mother, wife and children in this massacre, Geronimo vowed to kill as many white men as possible. For thirty years, he did a very good job at keeping this oath.

As a medicine man, but not a chief, he was given a position of prominence within the other tribes. Using this fame, he built a large band of personal followers. In the 1870s, the U.S. government began forcibly moving Native Americans onto reservations. Geronimo took his band and began to fight back.

For many years, Geronimo and his raiders hid between reservations and the Mexican desert. They raided Arizona, New Mexico and northern Mexico. His band became legendary, and he was the most feared Apache in the West. Bounties began to mount, and even more troops were brought in to try to capture them. Geronimo's raiding party proved to be highly elusive and remained free to hunt and raid for nearly a decade.

The U.S. Army, having exhausted most other methods, decided to turn other Apaches against Geronimo and hired five hundred scouts to find him. It did not take long for a few scouts to locate him and arrange for him to meet with army soldiers and commanders in Skeleton Canyon in 1886. General Miles met with Geronimo and arranged terms of surrender with the Indian to spare his men and their families.

Geronimo was famously quoted as saying, "I'm not going to bother anybody again. If you want to do anything to me, if you want to kill me, well that's all right. If you want to hang me, that's all right. Whatever you want to do, do it." When the general told Geronimo that he was not to be killed, the man replied, "If you are not going to kill me, get people good food, good water, good grass, good milk." The general explained to the Apache leader that he was too famous and too dangerous to be allowed to stay in the western United States. He was sending him and his people east, where nobody knew him and where he could do no further wrongs in the eyes of the army. General Miles was quoted as saying, "You will live a long life that way."

Within a few days, the entire Chiricahua tribe were put on trains bound for Florida to be held as prisoners. President Grover Cleveland ordered them sent to Fort Marion in St. Augustine, where many Indian prisoners had been sent in the previous Seminole Wars—including, at one point, the Seminole chief Osceola. They were ordered to be guarded with the "strictest vigilance."

Several important members of society in Pensacola had other plans for Geronimo and his people. They pleaded with their congressman to lobby to have Geronimo delivered to Fort Pickens instead of Fort Marion in St. Augustine, remembering what a boon to St. Augustine housing Chief Osceola had been. They used the logic that Fort Marion was too crowded and understaffed to handle such a dangerous group of Apaches. The army troops stationed at Fort Barrancas and Fort Pickens would be more than enough to guard Geronimo's infamous band.

With pressure from the congressman, President Cleveland quickly approved the petition, but for the Apache men only. He separated the families, breaking one of the promises made by General Miles at Geronimo's surrender in Skeleton Canyon. This enraged the Indians, but there was little they could do. The men were transported by train under guard toward Pensacola shortly thereafter.

In October 1886, Geronimo and fourteen of his warriors arrived at Fort Pickens. At first, he and his men were forced to work hard labor, which was also strongly against the agreements made at Skeleton Canyon. Another promise had been broken. Word quickly spread of the mistreatment of the Indians, and conditions improved slightly, as the city was planning to cash in on its new local celebrity.

An editorial in the *Pensacolian* newspaper stated upon Geronimo's arrival, "We welcome the nation's distinguished guests and promise to keep them safely under lock and key that they will forget their hair-raising proclivities and become good Indians."

By February 1887, the tourists had begun to flood to Pensacola from all over the country. The ferry from Pensacola carried them across the bay to Fort Pickens to view the prisoners. At fifty cents per head for adults

Geronimo and fellow Apache Indian prisoners on their way to Florida by train. Geronimo is in the front row and third from the right. 1886. *State Archives of Florida, Florida Memory.*

and twenty-five cents per child, the city began to rake in the money. Hundreds of people visited the fort to see the famous Geronimo and his braves in captivity.

Geronimo began to speak of all the promises made at his surrender that had been broken by President Cleveland and others. He was able to secure the reunion of his men with their families. Realizing his influence and celebrity status, he was able to leverage a few more benefits for himself and his people.

It wasn't long before Geronimo and his people were sent to other areas of incarceration. Even with some new freedoms, they remained prisoners. The band was separated and sent to several different reservations in multiple territories.

When Geronimo was sent off to begin touring as almost a sideshow attraction for the U.S. government, the city of Pensacola was devastated. It had lost one of its greatest tourist attractions. Geronimo had brought

Costumed woman standing in front of Geronimo's cell, Fiesta of Five Flags, Pensacola, Florida. 1955. *Johnson, Francis P., State Archives of Florida, Florida Memory.*

hundreds of visitors daily to the city and had been a great source of income. Now he was being sent on his way.

Geronimo went on to visit the St. Louis World's Fair in 1904. He spoke of making quite a bit of money signing autographs and posing for pictures. He also rode in the inaugural parade of President Theodore Roosevelt, who had admired the once proud medicine man. He died at Fort Sill, Oklahoma, in 1909. His people, the Chiricahuas, did not leave captivity until 1913.

As Geronimo neared death, he spoke of regrets. His last words were, "I should never have surrendered. I should have fought until I was the last man alive."

Fort Pickens would continue to be used until well after World War II. It was continuously upgraded. New cannons were installed as World War II began. Although the fort never saw an active battle after the Civil War, most say that the fort's mere existence was the major deterrent from any further attacks. The naval yard became the Pensacola Naval Base, and Fort Pickens became a state park.

Although Geronimo had left, the folks of Pensacola used his legacy to continue to bring tourists to the fort. His cell was labeled with a big sign, and tours were given to promote the history of the fort. To this day, you can visit the fort and see his old cell. When you visit, take a moment to offer respect for those who have passed and for a dark time in our history, now forever etched into the stone walls of Fort Pickens.

THE SECOND RIP VAN WINKLE
AND THE FLORIDA CAVERNS, MARIANNA

Just shy of 40 million years ago, the sea levels of the world were much higher than they are today. Most of what is now the southeastern United States coastal areas were submerged. Coral, shells and sediments accumulated on the seabed. When the sea levels receded, these sediments hardened into limestone bedrock.

This stratum is the foundation of much of the Florida peninsula. About 1 million years ago, acidic groundwater began to dissolve some of this limestone basin to form crevices that would allow rainwater to refill the state's precious aquifer, which lies just below the limestone. This aquifer provides most of Florida's drinking water supply.

Sinkholes are the most common landform caused by this erosion. "Karst" is the generic term used to describe land caused by this erosional process. Many other types of terrain can be created from this process, including disappearing streams, springs, underground drainage systems and caves.

With this geology in mind, Dr. J.C. Patterson of Malone, Florida, was on holiday in Virginia in the early 1930s. He visited the Luray Caverns. He immediately realized the potential of a cavern-focused state park in his home of Florida. He returned to the area and purchased nearly five hundred acres in North Florida that had been known to house small caves and an amazing natural bridge over the Chipola River.

The early European explorers learned from the Native Americans of the natural bridge of the Chipola River. Most were far more excited about this easy path across the river than they were about the small caves nearby. The Chacato Indians used a trail along this bridge for many years.

The Spanish military famously crossed the bridge in 1676 to raid a nearby fortified Chisca Indian village. One report from the journal of a 1693 Spanish exploratory expedition remarked that the river must have been very high at the time of the crossing, as the bridge was muddy and much more difficult to cross than had ever been reported. This implied that the bridge was used often by early Spanish explorers of the North American continent.

Since little is discussed in early documentation of the European exploration of Florida about the area, the existence of the nearby caves was obviously known. However, they were small and of little consequence to most of these travelers. In truth, archaeological discoveries of pottery shards and mammoth footprints in several caves predate all their writings by a great many years. The caves in the area were more important than these early explorers realized.

One cave that is now off limits to tourists is called Indian Cave. It had been used by ancient peoples as a shelter from the storms of the area. It was also possibly used for cold storage to keep food from spoiling in the humid Florida summers. Archaeologists have found numerous prehistoric items near the mouths of all the caves in the area. They don't believe the early inhabitants lived in the caves, but they did hold some significance in their lives.

More early history of the caverns includes a Spanish missionary named Friar Barreda delivering a Christian sermon to a local tribe surrounded by a beautiful underground cavern of wondrous beauty. During the construction of the modern-day park's visitors' center parking lot, a village site was found that corroborated this story.

The Indian Cave figured in many of the early European military engagements throughout the nineteenth century. In 1818, during what is now known as the First Seminole War, Andrew Jackson's army used the natural bridge to drive the Native Americans out of the area. There are legends that many Indians hid in the cave to avoid clashing with this force of invaders. During the Civil War, members of both the Union and Confederacy sought out the caves as a potential source of niter for gunpowder. As these caves were very damp, they were quickly deemed useless for this purpose.

During the antebellum years, the caves became a popular place to spend an afternoon for the population of the nearby city of Marianna. One legend from this era is too remarkable to not mention here. A group of local teens was out having a picnic near the natural bridge. Afterward, the teens went to explore the underground caves in the dark by feeling their way around without torches. It was a fun way to pass the time. It was also a chance to steal some private time with your partner away from the prying eyes of others.

On one such visit, a man apparently became fascinated by the walls' composition and began to tap on the walls of Indian Cave. One sounded hollow, giving off a slight echo behind it, so he tapped harder. He and his party were shocked when the wall gave way and revealed a previously undiscovered room of the caverns.

Once the dust cleared and their eyes readjusted to the darkness, they spotted an old man lying on the floor of the newly opened area. Fearing that they had opened some burial chamber or tomb, most backed away. The man bolted upright. He seemed as genuinely shocked to see them as they were to have found him.

The tale says that he spoke with a strange accent with a strong Spanish influence. He was wearing animal skins, a long beard and a cap similar to a coonskin cap the old settlers used to wear. Every one of the witnesses remembered that he had a very large bowie knife, which he brandished to keep them from approaching too closely.

The crowd of picnicking young people soon started to understand his method of talking and thick accent. He asked them simply what year it was. When they told him the year, he was said to have exclaimed, "I been sleep a hundred years!" Then he ran out the door of the cave, never to be seen again.

Now known as the "Second Rip Van Winkle," it was this legend and the historical anecdotes of the caves that many believe drove Dr. J.C. Patterson to buy all the land and dream of opening a park of caves in Florida. There was still the problem of how to build the park.

As the area was suffering through the Great Depression, Dr. Patterson had envisioned the cave park becoming a boon to the local economy, just as he had witnessed the caves in Luray, Virginia, being to their nearby community. He worked with Tom Yancy of the Marianna Chamber of Commerce, and together they got the area around the caves to be declared as Florida's seventh state park.

As part of Franklin D. Roosevelt's New Deal for America to help provide jobs for young men who had difficulty finding jobs, the Civilian Conservation Corps (CCC) was founded. The CCC provided unskilled manual labor jobs that assisted the conservation and development of natural resources found in rural lands owned by state, local and federal governments. These young men were given thirty dollars per month and room and board to assist in these efforts, most of which had to be sent back to their families at home.

This program quickly became the most popular of all the New Deal programs. The CCC planted nearly 3 billion trees to help reforest America. Its youthful workers built recreational facilities and trails in more than eight hundred parks nationwide. Although segregated, they had separate programs for African Americans and Native Americans, with equal pay but, sadly, as was common in those times, not equal treatment.

It was this influx of park money and workforce that Dr. Patterson needed to see his dream come alive. The CCC workers began to build trails and even a golf course along the Chipola River. The caves proved tough to gain proper access, but Patterson felt they would be enough of a draw for tourists even if they were a tad inaccessible.

In March 1937, a government surveyor named Olivier Chalifeaux went out after a terrible storm had passed through the park. He noticed a downed tree. Its root system had been ripped up, exposing a new cavern. He crawled into the hole and discovered what is now known as the Tour Cave. The cave was full of impressive underground rock features.

One of the amazing rock formations within the Florida Caverns. *Author's photo.*

Using only pickaxes and hand tools, the CCC formed a small subgroup of excavators called the "gopher gang." This gang of excavators became a fixture of Marianna folklore. Its exploits are told again and again as tourists visit the nearly four underground acres of caverns that the gang's hard work helped craft. The visitors' center at the park has numerous exhibits and photographs to help tourists learn the history of the CCC and the men who first crawled into Tour Cave.

Today, you can visit the park and see the extraordinary underground formations of stalagmites and stalactites. Extremely still underground pools of water and breathtaking vistas surround you, as park rangers host guided tours full of the natural and cultural history of the park. Unlike many cave tours elsewhere, here you are inches away from some of the breathtaking underground scenery. There is also a cavern at the park called Tunnel Cave that you can crawl into on your own with a flashlight for a less guided experience.

There are more than thirty other caves, including Indian Cave, which are off limits to the public. This is mostly due to this area being the home to a very endangered and sadly possibly extinct species of bat and other very rare forms of life within the unique ecosystem of the caves.

So, when visiting North Florida, if you need a day away from the beaches, make a stop at the Florida Caverns. Give thanks at the statue dedicated to the CCC workers who built the park. Maybe enjoy a round at the Depression-era golf course the workers built. Then get a glimpse at an underground world filled with history and legend. Be sure to keep an eye out for any sleepy, coonskin-wearing fellows with a knife, though, if you stumble into another unknown chamber.

THE DEVIL'S SCHOOL, JACKSONVILLE

Right in the heart of downtown Jacksonville stands a very impressive and intimidating building. The roof nearly touches the I-95 and I-10 junction overpass that runs through the city. At rush hour, gridlock grinds traffic to a near standstill at the junction more often than not.

People stuck in the snarling traffic jams that are so frequent here can't help but look over at this incredible brick building with giant columns. They must wonder how such an ominous and obviously long-abandoned building still sits so silent, so idle and so malevolent. Surely the devil himself must have something to do with it still standing and resisting the expansive nature of the surrounding, bustling city. Very few know the true identity of the building.

Long ago, these grounds were the home of Riverside Park School. It was a small wooden schoolhouse built in 1891. Several additions were built over the years as Jacksonville became a huge population center. It was considered by many to be a great fire hazard and eventually was marked for replacement.

In 1915, voters of Duvall County passed an unheard-of $1 million bond to build more than a dozen new schoolhouses out of brick in the county. The one where Riverside Park was located would be called Public School No. 4. Construction started in 1917, and Florida Engineering and Construction built and completed it in 1918 at a cost of just over $250,000. The school overlooked Riverside Park and jutted against the St. Johns River.

The Neoclassical architecture of the school makes it quite impressive. The portico at the front of the school is supported by four massive Doric

Public School No. 4 right under I-95 in downtown Jacksonville. *Author's photo.*

columns. The building had an interconnected auditorium and cafeteria and held rooms for numerous classes. The school was built to last one hundred years.

So, why did it close in 1960, just over forty years later? Why are there unsubstantiated rumors of it being a Catholic school in the late 1960s or early 1970s? It was known to house offices and storage for the City of Jacksonville for a short time before the building was condemned and abandoned. Most everything else about the school's later years seemed shrouded in mystery.

Shortly after opening, the school was renamed for a long-serving faculty member and former school principal, Annie Lytle. The school was used by many students and has scores of alumni. The stories begin near the end of the active days of the school. Some of these legends are simply over the top.

The most famous legend of this school is that there was a huge furnace in the school that exploded sometime in the late 1960s. This explosion allegedly killed hundreds of students and several faculty members. It is simply amazing that such an incredible explosion never made it into any newspapers or reports of the time. The origin of this legend appears to come from a fire in the building in 1995 that caused the collapse of a large portion of the roof. It had been set by vagrants using the long-abandoned property.

The next story about the school is that the crazed janitor of the school went on a killing spree among the students. He had apparently been an axe-murderer who had changed his name to get the job at the school. One day, he simply cracked and assaulted several students. The hallways were reportedly covered in blood. Some paranormal researchers have said that the ghosts of these victims can still be heard in the halls. It is unlikely that this would have gone unreported as well. Perhaps someone watched too many *Nightmare on Elm Street* movies and thought of the abandoned school.

Yet another legend of the school notes that the principal went insane at the school after having an affair with a student, who then threatened him with blackmail. He killed the young student, and to hide the crime, he cooked her. Then he served her for a faculty meeting. Once the staff had eaten, he then informed them of the deed and blackmailed them. The faculty became a demonic cannibal cult that would prey on students with no home life, or those they felt wouldn't be missed. Once caught, the school was closed for a few days, and a priest was brought in to exorcise the demons possessing the school. The school reopened for a short time as a private Catholic school, but the evil remained. It's curious how this, too, went unreported by any media organizations.

The truth of the school closure does not lie behind any of these myths. Like most things, the truth is rather simple. The construction of the new I-10 and I-95 junction was so close to the school that it almost touched the buildings. This proximity just made the school unusable.

The Annie Lytle School sat abandoned for years and became a gathering place of local homeless and drug addicts. Gangs and other groups often held initiations there. There is tons of graffiti covering the walls, with some being very satanic in their messages. This may have been the basis for some of the devilish legends.

In 1999, the school was bought and was intended to be demolished to make way for a new set of condominiums. By this time, more of the roof had collapsed, and the site was merely a place for urban explorers and amateur ghost hunters. A group of local history buffs got together and organized an attempt to get the school declared a historic landmark. It was granted this designation in 2000.

Today, the ruins of the Annie Lytle School are a long way off from the fancy brick and almost palatial feel it must have had when originally constructed. The halls, once covered in debris and graffiti, are slowly being restored by a group of dedicated volunteers intent on restoring the building so that it can be used again for some purpose at some point.

While trespassing is still strictly forbidden at the school, these volunteers at the Annie Lytle Preservation Group have been hard at work. The debris and grounds have been cleared and the school is in much better shape than it has been in years. What it will be used for in the future remains to be seen. You can help financially or physically in the restoration by contacting the Public School No. 4 Preservation Group (www.savepublicschoolnumber4.com).

THE BARDIN BOOGER AND DOGMEN, BARDIN

Just north of Palatka on Highway 17 and deep in the woods of Putnam County lies a little-known town called Bardin. It is a small town and has only one main intersection, where stands Bud's Grocery, at the heart of the town. Bud Key, the owner of this establishment, gladly posts an article in the window of his shop about the area's most famous inhabitant, "The Bardin Booger."

We covered Skunk Apes, also known as the Sasquatch of Florida, in our previous book, *Eerie Florida*. For those who missed it or need a refresher course, here's Skunk Ape 101. While most associate Bigfoot or Sasquatch with the great woods of the Northwest or the Appalachians, a great many sightings occur in the middle of Florida, particularly in the Green Swamp, the Ocala National Forest and in the Everglades. The sightings take place in all those dark spots with no roads when you look at a Florida map. These particular areas seem to house tales of large primate-like creatures with a terrible odor that smells of death and decay. So you can see, the Sunshine State has numerous sightings of many of these cryptozoological creatures.

The "Booger" in Bardin, however, predates many Sasquatch sightings. Most Skunk Ape sightings peaked in the '60s and '70s. One of the first sightings of this beast near Bardin we were able to find was from 1947. A woman out riding from Palatka spotted an odd-looking man on the side of the trail among the pines she was riding through. The man was very large and seemed to be wearing either a fur coat or a raincoat. This was very strange, as it was very warm and humid with clear skies. Her horse stopped

Bud's Grocery in Bardin is the official headquarters of Booger research. *Author's photo.*

in its tracks, as it smelled something off. The woman realized that it was no coat the man was wearing—he was covered in fur. She then saw it was not a man at all. It had a pig-like nose and clear-skinned face. The creature then rose to a full height, towering over her, even on horseback. It began to use the tree as a scratching post. She turned the horse around and fled home.

The creature was spotted again and again over the years. A sighting in the early 1970s told of the creature nearly seven feet tall with the "face of a caveman" simply watching a group as their truck raced by on the road. It held up an old oil lantern as it turned and walked into the woods, disappearing almost as soon as it entered the tree line, as though it blended into the woods. The astonished passengers then saw the light of the lantern fade away as well.

While most stories differ about the creature, a few things are consistent. The first detail is that the furry giant usually holds a lantern, which sets him far apart from the usual Skunk Ape sightings of the state. Secondly, he tends to shy away from the public. Finally, he usually likes to relax by a nearby creek.

In 1981, the *Palatka Daily News* had a very slow news week and decided to run a story on the Bardin creature. Jody Delzell, the publisher, was said to have called it the "Bardin Booger," with "Booger" being a shortened version of "Boogieman." The column was a huge success, and suddenly the little town of Bardin, with a population of fewer than four hundred, received

The Bardin Booger with his lantern. *Illustration by Kari Schultz.*

international exposure when the Associated Press picked up the story and syndicated it worldwide.

Cryptid hunters and monster enthusiasts flooded the town, and the number of sightings hiked up considerably. Bud's Grocery became the central headquarters for all the hunters hoping to get that significant bit of evidence to prove the monster's existence to the world. Bud, his wife and his daughter began to stock Bardin Booger T-shirts and other crazy items. They hung the first story up in the front window and maintained a "Booger File" with all the news clippings they could gather.

Jody Delzell took the Booger and made his own news column in which he gave satirical opinions on matters that Delzell couldn't write as his own. Dezell created a character called "Boog" for his column. He was an ancient wandering inhabitant of old Florida trying to get by in the modern society and world. He would use these stories to comment on political and societal changes from a sense of history of the area. They proved to be immensely popular.

These stories led Bardin's Billy and Lena Crain to make a homemade Bardin Booger outfit (complete with lantern) from a gorilla costume. They would show up at events in town and even the local area schools. They would perform Billy's fantastic song, "The Bardin Booger":

> *Mr. Bardin Booger, Bardin is your home*
> *And every day, you love to roam*
> *Runnin' through the bushes and runnin' through the trees,*
> *Mr. Bardin Booger, don't you get me, please.*

They followed that hit up with "The Bardin Booger's Christmas Wish." The Crains toured parades and other events for many years until Billy's passing in 1992. Lena Crain still plays a recorded version of the song and reportedly still suits up in the modified gorilla costume in which they used to make appearances.

In private interviews, Bud Key admitted to enhancing the legends of the Booger and even having a costumed individual run through the woods at one point to drum up further business. When the local sheriff told him to cut it out or someone might get shot, he and his accomplices did so. He gladly admits, though, that most of the sightings were well before they tried to cash in.

Recently, however, there has been a new twist on this old legend. A more recent phenomenon is spreading like wildfire throughout the cryptid community. This new creature looks more like the werewolves of Hollywood than the Bigfoot of old. These beasts are also much smarter and even hunt in packs. They are the Dogmen.

While many point out that these new creatures only began to appear after makeup special effects became more readily available, Dogman legends may date back much earlier. Sally Gage—an anthropologist, lycanthropologist and descendant of the Anishinaabe tribe of Native Americans—loves to point something out to those who have only seen the modern spike in reports. Primarily, she explained that early Native American art depicts numerous wolf-men images in ancient drawings. While many of these images are associated with manitou or other Indian creatures of folklore, more and more believe that these might involve Native American interaction with the Dogmen dating before recorded history.

The Dogman looked like a "freaking werewolf from the movies." *Illustration by Kari Schultz.*

While the bulk of these sightings are from Michigan and the Manistee National Forest, there have been sightings from all over North America. And now, just like Sasquatch, Florida has its own sightings of the infamous Dogmen. Some recent sightings of these creatures include the area around Bardin. These have spurred renewed interest in the old legends. The hunt is on again.

One recent encounter near Bardin involved a young deer hunter who had bagged a large buck and was bringing him into a check station. He had stopped in the woods to attend "nature's call." Then he heard a strange growling sound from behind him. Thinking it was a bear smelling the fresh kill, he reached for his rifle. Seeing the giant hairy arm reach up into the bed of his raised truck confirmed his suspicions, and he quickly reached into the cab to grab his gun. The creature then rose up from behind the truck. It stood nearly 9 feet tall, with a protruding snout, pointed ears and long, straight hair covering its entire form.

"It looked just like a freaking werewolf from the movies," claimed the witness. He tried to fire his weapon, but the intense smell the creature exuded and (he admitted later) an overwhelming sense of fear caused him to miss the shot. The creature ran off at the sound and disappeared into the thick brush in seconds. The man decided to dedicate his life to hunting this creature. He wishes to remain anonymous until he can "bag the big one" and prove his story. He also feels that he was being watched by other creatures in the area at the time of his encounter.

While these "upright canine" or Dogmen stories become more and more common, can we be sure it is all just the work of pranksters? Many, like Sally Gage, believe that it is merely the matter of our population encroaching on their living space and hunting grounds. As more and more forest area is being taken away to make room for more housing for the ever-growing population of Florida, it is inevitable that encounters with all sorts of cryptid creatures will increase in frequency. Hopefully one day we will have that final definitive answer as to what is out there.

In the meantime, the Booger still roams and relaxes by the creek as he carries his lantern. He lives on in the tales, history and folklore of the little North Florida town of Bardin.

THE HEAD OF OSCEOLA AND THE GHOSTS
OF THE OLDEST CITY, ST. AUGUSTINE

S t. Augustine is the oldest continuously inhabited city in the United States. It predates Plymouth Rock by about sixty years. The Spanish settlement here has enough history for several dozen books. Ghosts and spooky stories are so common here that there are almost more haunted tours in this city than in Charleston, South Carolina, and Savannah, Georgia, combined. It is perhaps only eclipsed in the United States by the number of ghost tours of New Orleans. There are numerous books from The History Press telling these tales, and even just listing the stories, their locations would fill several volumes. The town has quite the monopoly on paranormal hotspots.

While ghost stories and legends are nothing new to the town, the ghost tour industry is still relatively recent to the Ancient City's scene. Most of these tours developed during the 1980s and '90s, when local tour guides noticed a surge in interest in the paranormal—when shows like *The X-Files* and horror movies were dominating home video. The supernatural was becoming big business. The historic tours already prevalent in the area began to delve deeper and deeper into the stories of the strange, macabre and ghostly history of the city. One of the founding fathers of this wave of tours was Doug Stenroos, now known as "the Sheriff."

The Sheriff's Ghost Walk is the longest-running walking ghost tour in the town, and for six nights a week, the Sheriff will deputize you and take you through the streets and alleys of the historic district of downtown St. Augustine. He is a fantastic storyteller who regales you with numerous ghostly and eerie tales of his home city. While there are trolley rides and more modern types of tours in the area that offer their own unique experiences, you are hard-pressed to get more bang for your buck than with the Sheriff.

One of the best stories he tells is that of the ghost of Judge Stickney. To understand this legend, you have to learn about the Huguenot Cemetery, which lies just outside the old city gates of St. Augustine. The city was once the walled Spanish City, with the large and impressive Castillo de San Marco fortress built close by to guard the bay. When Florida joined the United States, the fort and walled city became a hub of port activity in the new state.

St. Augustine was still a predominately Catholic city under the Spanish. This meant there were two cemeteries. The older Tolomato Cemetery inside the city walls had once been a Native American Indian ground and now housed the Catholic dead. A new cemetery had been built outside the city walls to accommodate those not of the Catholic faith. This graveyard was called the Huguenot Cemetery and opened just in time to handle the numerous victims of a yellow fever outbreak that decimated the population of the town.

The Castillo de San Marco was once Fort Marion, where Osceola and many other Native Americans were held. *Author's photo.*

Before closing in the late 1800s with a severely overstuffed graveyard, Huguenot had more than 436 recorded burials. There are far fewer markers in the cemetery. It is also estimated that there are even more significant numbers of buried dead there that went unrecorded. No wonder so many of the tours stop here to tell tales of the numerous ghosts that haunt the cemetery.

During the Civil War, a lawyer from Washington, D.C., came down to Florida. John B. Stickney settled in St. Augustine, became a local attorney and began to dabble in politics. It didn't take long for people to start calling him a "Carpetbagger." Despite this label, he quickly became a very prominent figure in the town and was appointed as a judge not long after the end of the Civil War.

Stickney continued to pursue politics, and his business ventures back in his original home in Washington, D.C. Many of his family grew tired of St. Augustine, and they moved north to help run his interests back in the nation's capital. Now a local judge in St. Augustine, he would frequently travel the rail lines back and forth between both cities. He would often make campaign stops and speeches for various national and state politicians to help further his own interests and political aspirations.

During one such trip to D.C. in 1882, Stickney fell ill and died. His body was returned to St. Augustine to be buried in the town where he had grown to prominence. He was laid to rest at Huguenot Cemetery with much fanfare. An impressive marker was placed at his grave. This chess piece–like monument is just as remarkable today as it was when first erected, but Judge Stickney's story doesn't end here.

Twenty years passed, and Stickney's children had by now all moved to Washington. They decided to have their father's body disinterred and reburied near them in D.C., and a gravedigger was hired. The proper notices were placed in and around the city and its newspapers. Naturally, the digging up of the grave of Judge John Stickney was going to be quite the spectacle. Nearly the entire town showed up to watch.

The stories diverge here, but the consensus is that when he was dug up and the casket opened, Judge Stickney's body was remarkably well preserved. The most impressive thing that wowed the onlookers was the flash of his gold teeth. A few drunken observers charged the casket. They smashed in the judge's face and ran off with the gold teeth. Today, Stickney lies reinterred up in Washington, D.C. The Sheriff and most other tours, however, love talking about the ghost of Judge Stickney, with his stovetop pipe, searching the grounds of Huguenot looking for his gold teeth.

Above: Judge Stickney's impressive grave marker at the Huguenot Cemetery in St. Augustine. *Author's photo.*

Opposite: The ghost of Judge Stickney is frequently reported as looking for his lost teeth among the tombstones of the Huguenot Cemetery. *Illustration by Kari Schultz.*

After this stop, the Sheriff will then walk you through the old city gates and tell tales of ghosts we covered a bit in *Eerie Florida*. He will then draw your attention to the marvelous Castillo de San Marco across the way. The old fort built by the Spanish using coquina, a shell and concrete mixture, still stands strong on the bay. This fort has weathered English attacks, French attacks and pirate attacks. It was renamed Fort Marion during the Civil War and used for defense.

Confederate troops seized the fort during the Civil War, as it was already nearing its 300th birthday on January 7, 1861. With an impressive haul of guns and artillery, the fort protected the city for a short while from Union forces. This did not last long, as by March 1862 the fort had fallen to Union forces as they began to concentrate their efforts to gain control of all the ports along the Florida coastline.

All of this is secondary to the dark history of Fort Marion. During the 1830s, many Native Americans in Florida attempted to resist the U.S. Army's efforts to forcibly relocate them to a reservation west of the Mississippi River. The Seminole Wars were the longest and bloodiest Indian wars fought by the United States, with more than two thousand soldiers and unknown numbers of Native Americans slain. Fort Marion became a prisoner of war camp for many of the captured natives. One prisoner held there was the great Seminole warrior named Osceola.

Osceola's early history is as much legend as was the rest of his life. Most historians agree that he was born somewhere in Alabama around 1804 to a Creek Indian mother and a Scottish father. He went by the name Billy Powell, but as he grew older, he embraced his native heritage and joined his adopted tribe of the Seminole Indians. The Seminoles were mostly refugees of many of the southeastern tribes. Osceola and his mother were involved in the Creek War of 1813–14 and traveled to then Spanish-held Florida, where the Seminole tribe took them in.

This, sadly, did not prove to be the respite from U.S. oppression they sought, for soon Spain gave Florida to the United States in 1819 with the signing of the Adams-Onis Treaty. Just a few years later, with the signing of the Treaty of Moultrie Creek in 1823, the Seminole Indians agreed to give up their claims of land in Florida.

It was somewhere around this time that young Billy Powell acquired the name of Osceola. The name translates as "black drink singer." Most historians agree that this comes from a rite of the Seminoles in which young warriors would drink a black liquid brewed from yaupon holly leaves. Osceola must have completed the ritual of drinking the foul liquid, which usually causes a violent purge of the stomach, with a "warrior's song" instead of retching.

In 1830, President Andrew Jackson signed the Indian Removal Act. By 1838, federal legislation required the removal of all Cherokee, Creek, Choctaw, Chickasaw and Seminole tribes, to be moved to the newly created Indian Territory in what is now Oklahoma. Many of the Seminoles had been refugees from the Creek War and wanted nothing to do with this forced relocation. Many had even fought against some rival tribes being placed in this territory, including the Creeks. Most Seminole chiefs refused to sign the treaty, which led to the outbreak of the Second Seminole War.

Osceola became quite a famous leader of his people during this time. As an accomplished tactician, he led his tribe to victory over General Duncan Clinch at the Battle of Withlacoochee in December 1835. He directed numerous successful ambushes and relocated his followers, including many noncombatants, to safe havens multiple times. The army seemed to have no luck in finding Osceola or his people.

General Thomas Jessup arranged to meet with Osceola under a flag of truce near St. Augustine. Once there, the army officers seized the warrior and his men and imprisoned them. Many were relieved at the capture of this outlandish warrior, but public outcry over using such a dishonorable act by Jessup would backfire in much of the press. Sentiment for the Indian plight grew among the American populace.

In Fort Marion, Osceola became a tourist attraction. Visitors to the fort would want to watch and speak with the great warrior. He began to fall into ill health. This was most likely due to the captivity and the numerous visitors. His fame, though, was still spreading.

A young Baltimore-trained surgeon named Dr. Fredrick Weedon, who had recently ended his enlistment in the Florida militia, was called to the fort to help with the ill soldiers in Fort Marion. Malaria and other diseases were common among the troops. Most of these illnesses were lumped into what many locals simply called the "Florida Fever." Doctor Weedon helped treat the soldiers stationed at the fort. He also began to treat its most famous captive, Osceola.

In December 1837, about 20 of the captured warriors in Fort Marion escaped their cells and climbed over the walls. Osceola was too weak and too ill to escape. All 237 Indians left in the fort, including Osceola, would be immediately transferred. Weedon would be one of several doctors sent with the prisoners to Fort Moultrie on Sullivan's Inland near Charleston, South Carolina.

A torrent of artists and visitors came to see the Indian leader before he left St. Augustine. Though very ill, Osceola selected several elaborate costumes and posed for many pictures and paintings. He continued this even after his arrival in South Carolina.

Per Weedon's diary, he held numerous conversations with Osceola in the weeks leading up to his death. Osceola told him that he wished he could have accepted his treatments, but the prophets of his people were the only care he could receive. Noted portrait artist George Catlin came around this time to paint Osceola, and this painting would later travel the world and tour all the most renowned galleries of Europe.

When Osceola died, a death-cast was made of his head by Dr. Benjamin Strobel that is still on display at the Smithsonian Institution. It was sometime after this that Dr. Weedon decided to remove the head of his deceased patient for some bizarre souvenir. In his diary, he often expressed a genuine empathy for the plight of the Seminoles. However, his writings also showed a typical-for-the-time cultural bias against the Indians. This may explain why he was so readily able to remove the head of one he often called a friend.

Weedon kept the souvenir a secret until he returned home to St. Augustine. The doctor displayed the head in his drugstore. Letters from officers who

Chief Osceola. 18--. *State Archives of Florida, Florida Memory.*

had served at both Fort Marion and Fort Moultrie confirmed that the head was indeed Osceola's.

Stories from the Weedon children claimed that the doctor would leave the head on the bedpost of his children at night. He would lock them in their room with it when he felt they needed discipline. The head stayed with the family for a long while. Dr. Weedon eventually gave it to his son as a wedding present.

When Weedon died, his son gave the head to his mentor, Dr. Valentine Mott. Mott kept the head closely guarded out of fear of it being stolen. He eventually donated the head to the Medical College of the City of New York. A fire at the college in 1866 marked the last time anyone saw the head, and it was presumed destroyed in the blaze.

Only recently did National Park Service officials allow the examination of the grave of Osceola just outside Fort Moultrie. They did uncover a headless skeleton, confirming the long-held belief that Dr. Weedon really did own the head of the once proud Seminole warrior.

At this point, most ghost tours will direct you to the many haunted bed-and-breakfast inns of the town. They might even lead you to a ghostly pub or tavern in which you could drink some fine spirits with the spiritual inhabitants that might be lurking within the bar. The Sheriff often ends his walk with some audience participation from a friendly local ghost and sends you off to enjoy the rest of the town.

Many tourists want more than a few stories. The draw of the ghoulish will lead them to such locations as Ripley's Believe It or Not! Museum in the old Warden Castle near the Castillo de San Marco. Old Fort Marion has now returned to its original Spanish nomenclature. Many will cross the Bridge of Lions to visit the haunted St. Augustine Lighthouse across the harbor from the fort. Others will seek out some of the more unusual offerings of the town.

One of the most interesting places in town is Wolfe's Museum of Mystery on Charlotte Street in St. Augustine. This incredible establishment lies just off the main shopping thoroughfare of St. George Street. It is the home of the wonderful Wolfgang Von Mentz and houses his collection of oddities, rare art, antiques and more zaniness than you will ever find under one roof. Almost every single one of the pieces on display is for sale, and the five-dollar entrance fee (as of this writing) is usable toward the purchase of any of the artifacts inside.

Galleries tend to rotate at the museum but currently include a dead Sasquatch, Marie Laveau's altar, a Cannibal Kitchen and a Lizzie Borden

Left: Outside of Wolfe's Museum of Mystery in St. Augustine. *Author's photo.*

Below: A scene inside the Medieval Torture Museum of St. Augustine. *Author's photo.*

room. There is a horror movie–themed room you can rent for viewing parties. Truly, Wolfe's is a unique place in a unique town for those with a great sense for the macabre.

Another new, not-for-the-squeamish attraction in St. Augustine is the Medieval Torture Museum. A private collection of replicas and original implements of terror fills this museum just above the family-friendly St. George Street. While some liberties are taken with the history of some of these exhibits, the general sense of dread is palpable. Hundreds of implements of torture fill the large museum, with several rooms dedicated to diverse eras, including the Inquisition and the Witch Trials. The collection is full of torment-inducing tools of madmen and tyrants. You can't help but get chills as you are drawn into the world of darkness that the exhibits showcase.

Within the Ancient City, there is plenty of colorful history and so much wonderful food and culture. St. Augustine is a place to not be missed during any Florida visit. While there, keep your eyes peeled for any possible ghostly encounters. Keep your ears open for any spooky legends. If you drop by Wolfe's or the Torture Museum, or maybe take a walk with the Sheriff, make sure you tell them *Freaky Florida* sent you.

THE OLDER CITY, NEW SMYRNA BEACH

Ask anybody what the oldest continuously inhabited city in the United States is and you might get some Plymouth Rock answers. Mostly, you'll get St. Augustine, which may not be the right answer after all. Thanks to an unusual set of ruins, some historians believe that the quirky seaside community of New Smyrna Beach may be the true oldest city. Some even believe that Old Fort Park may have been the original St. Augustine.

Spain first explored the land they called La Florida in the 1500s and made several colonies. The most successful of these was the port at St. Augustine. The Spanish found the Florida peninsula to be a hard place to colonize. The heat, bugs, disease and aggressive Native Americans made the task of colonization nearly impossible. When a successful colony was set up, it was fortified quickly. Unable to find useful stone, the Spanish reverted to coquina, a mixture of limestone and broken seashells, which they were familiar with from their own coast. This is the primary construction material used in the famous Castillo de San Marco in St. Augustine.

The Seven Years' War between Britain, France and Spain erupted across Europe, and of course, it bled into their colonies in the New World. The fighting was especially brutal in what is now Georgia. Florida had its share of battles, but nothing on the scale of some of the fighting to the north. The Spanish lost Florida to the British after signing the First Treaty of Paris in February 1763. The Spanish packed up and moved to Cuba.

The British sent many settlers and supplies to the old Spanish forts to secure their new colony. Dr. Andrew Turnbull from Scotland recruited more than 1,400 colonists and eight ships to establish a new settlement in Florida. His group was built with settlers from the Mediterranean, with mostly Minorcan, Italian, Greek and Corsican colonists. Gracia Dura Bin, Turnbull's wife, was from Asia Minor, and her home was Smyrna. The new colony was founded as New Smyrna. Only a little over 1,200 survived the trip to their new home in Florida.

The colony did not fare well. Supplies were only enough for a few hundred. Disease, Indians, the oppressive heat and the lack of food storage combined to decimate the population quickly. Within the decade, fewer than five hundred were still living and working the lands near New Smyrna. Most fled north to St. Augustine. Turnbull had built his home on a strange foundation of stones near the shore. It was destroyed sometime before the Spanish regained Florida.

The confusion about the history of the strange stone ruins began even earlier. On a map from 1605 drawn by Albero Mexia, a Spanish soldier from St. Augustine, the area here was marked as the home of an Ais Indian village called Caparaca. Some historians claim that the ruins of Turnbull's colony may have been built on a preexisting shell midden that may have been left from the village of Caparaca. Famous naturalist William Bartram wrote about the mound in the area in his reports but mentioned no stone structure on it in the mid-1770s.

There is some historical evidence stating that in 1776, workers traveled from St. Augustine and went to New Smyrna to see a large stone building being constructed there. Work was apparently finished on this structure as the colonists returned to St. Augustine. Some claim that the building in question was Turnbull's unfinished home. All we know is that in 1778, the colony collapsed, and Turnbull and his family moved to Charleston, South Carolina. The site then sat abandoned for many years.

The Spanish once again regained control of Florida in 1783 after the American Revolution and the Treaty of Paris. This time, however, most of the current British settlers did not leave Florida, and the Spanish didn't send many new colonists to their old colony. Dr. Ambrose Hull of Connecticut was offered a grant of land in this area by the Spanish in 1801. Hull arrived in New Smyrna and began a plantation for sugar and cotton. He named the site of the strange stone ruins Mount Olive, as there were olive trees growing near it that must have been planted by the Turnbull colony.

Ambrose Hull decided to build his home on the stone foundation he found there. Stonemasons were recruited in 1805 to build his home. He used an existing coquina foundation to build his large house. No one is exactly sure

The ruins at Smyrna Beach date back farther than anticipated. *Author's photo.*

what it looked like, but it was said to have had turrets, towers and multiple floors. We do know that it was destroyed during the War of 1812 by the British. Again, the site went unused for many years.

John D. Sheldon later built a hotel on the site in the 1850s. This large structure housed many of Florida's elite and finest of the period. The hotel suffered the same fate as the previous buildings at this location. It was destroyed during the Civil War.

No one is completely sure how old the foundation is. Was it merely the foundation for Turnbull's home from the 1700s? Is it some forgotten colony of the Spanish, as the coquina construction suggests? We will never truly know for sure, as coquina is notoriously hard to date. With so much construction above and into the original foundation, even the original design and shape is lost to antiquity.

With no conclusive evidence, St. Augustine is still safe in claiming to be the oldest continuously inhabited city in the United States. The historians will continue arguing, though, that New Smyrna might give it a run for its money. When visiting the town, make sure to stop by Old Fort Park and visit a unique historical mystery that could only exist in Freaky Florida.

THE I-4 DEAD ZONE, LAKE MONROE

Many people visit Florida by airplane in every size and shape, from the small private planes to the big jumbo jets. Some tourists come via train. Quite a few visitors come by boat, also ranging in size from the tiniest sailboat to the large cruise ships. The bulk of Florida travelers, however, come by automobile.

Most of these tourists drive in on the main interstates that cut through the state. I-95 mirrors the famous US-1 Highway along the eastern Atlantic coast of Florida. I-75 is more central but does follow the Gulf Coast for a great deal in the South. These roads have one major joining interstate right across the middle of the Florida peninsula. That road is I-4, which many say is cursed.

Since 1963, more than 2,500 accidents have occurred in a small quarter-mile section of I-4, halfway between Orlando and Daytona. While close to Sanford and an even shorter drive to the psychic commune of Cassadaga, this stretch of I-4 is claimed by no city. It begins just past the Lake Monroe bridge over the St. John's River on the eastbound side of the interstate.

Why are there more accidents in this lone stretch rather than the rest of the interstate, which reaches from Tampa to Daytona? There's another level to this mystery, as this expanse of road had some of the worst hurricanes in memory pass right over it. Many observers of this dark history state that it is simply coincidence. There are others who say that the graves of four settlers lie under the overpass here and they are not resting in peace.

The St. Joseph's Catholic Colony was located on this spot in the 1880s. The colony was mostly filled with German and Dutch immigrants who were working the land in a series of farms in the area. As was common in that day, an outbreak of yellow fever ravaged the colony. One family was hit so hard that all four of them died within days. Since the priest of the colony had already died, there was no one to administer their last rites. The family had to be buried without ceremony on a small plot in their land.

The colony collapsed with so many deaths, and the graves fell into disrepair. In contrast, the nearby town of Lake Monroe began to grow. Sometime in the early 1900s, a farmer named Albert Hawkins purchased land in the surrounding area and began his own farm. When he stumbled on four graves, he fenced in the area and made it into a small cemetery, right in the middle of his fields. Sadly, time had already worn away all information on the wooden markers, and the family's names were lost to history.

The legend of the unearthed graves and their little cemetery in the middle of a field began to spread throughout the area. A famous early story of the graves is that a boy in the 1950s decided to sneak into the graveyard and damage the markers. He was apparently slain on the way home in what many thought was a hit and run, as no one was ever caught. One story states that some farmer asked to use Hawkins's farmland for his own use. He removed the fence around the graves with the intent of plowing even closer. That very night, the farmer's house burned to the ground.

Most in town felt that the entire Hawkins farm was haunted and avoided the property. The location became widely known as the "Field of the Dead." The Hawkins home burned down shortly after Albert tried to rebuild the fence around the graves. The Hawkins family moved away in 1959, when they sold their farm to the State of Florida for the construction of a new interstate.

Surveyors marked the graves for relocation. Plans began to take shape throughout the state, and the first segment of I-4 opened between Plant City and Lakeland. According to legend, the graves were never moved. As the area needed to be raised for the new highway, fill dirt was poured into the area and on top of those four lonely graves.

That very day, one of the worst hurricanes to hit the state in a generation was crossing the southern part of Florida. Hurricane Donna was of unprecedented force and on a direct path for Tampa Bay. Suddenly, the storm, now called "Deadly Donna," turned on a dime and headed northeast; it passed right over the graveyard. Most storms weaken once over the middle of the state and away from the waters of the Atlantic or Gulf of Mexico.

This stretch of I-4 has had more accidents and casualties than even some of the busiest interchanges in the state. *Sanford Historical Society.*

Donna never slowed down as it plowed right for the I-4 Dead Zone and Lake Monroe. The immense destruction of the storm delayed construction for weeks.

When the new section of road from Sanford to Daytona was finally opened to much fanfare in the mid-1960s, it did not take long for that section of road to earn the reputation that it still holds to this day. The first accident happened within hours of its opening when a large semi jackknifed, just above the graveyard's location. The number of accidents in the area since that fateful first one is staggering.

Even recently, when construction returned to the area, a successive series of hurricanes again changed direction and barreled down on the small overpass. The residents of nearby Sanford and Lake Monroe were hit hard by Hurricanes Bonnie and Charley in 2004. Construction was once again delayed for months to repair the damage these storms caused. The quick succession of storms caused the Weather Channel to air an episode of their series *American Super/Natural* all about the "I-4 Dead Zone" in 2014.

While delving into the numerous accidents, you'll find reports of mysterious lights and strange mists rising just before the crash. Strange electrical malfunctions cause brakes or engines to seize. Numerous drivers say they swerved to avoid people on the road when no one was there.

So, if you drive this section of road, pay extra care. As you cross Lake Monroe, keep your eyes open for Pinkie the Sea Monster, often spotted there, as we discussed in *Eerie Florida*. Beware of your radio and cellphone picking up strange and unusual voices. Dodge the ghostly hitchhikers and strange, quickly rising mists. Most of all, just be careful in the traffic that flows through here. You don't want to be another statistic for the I-4 Dead Zone.

GATOR JOE AND MA BARKER, OCKLAWAHA

Kate Barker was described by J. Edgar Hoover as "the most vicious, dangerous and resourceful criminal brain of the last decade." Kate, also known as "Arizona Barker" or simply "Ma Barker," was presented in numerous films, songs and books as a monstrous mother who controlled and organized the infamous Barker-Karpis gang out of Chicago, Illinois, and then later St. Paul, Minnesota. A nationwide manhunt for her ended in an obscure little town on the shores of Lake Weir, deep in the heart of Florida. It ended in the longest shootout in FBI history. All of this was thanks largely to a legendary gator that roamed the waters of Lake Weir in the small town of Ocklawaha.

Born Arizona Clark in Missouri in 1873, young "Arrie" lived with her family on a small farm. In 1892, she married George Barker, and they had four sons. Herman was born in 1893, Lloyd followed in 1897, Arthur arrived in 1899 and, finally, the Barkers added Fred to the family in 1901. Census records from the time show that the father, George Barker, worked a variety of jobs from farming to station engineer and even a watchman. Sadly, it seems that the Barkers were too poor to educate their sons very much.

By 1910, their eldest son, Herman, had already been arrested for highway robbery. The heinousness of the crime was added to when he ran over a child in the getaway car. During the next few years, Herman and his brothers kept increasing the audacity of their crimes, which included robbery, kidnapping and murder. Their reputation led them to be noticed by the Central Park gang, which marked their recruitment into a major crime syndicate.

During the late 1920s, Arrie and George split up. There are different versions as to the reasons for their separation. Some say George left because he couldn't deal with his family's life of crime. A family friend once said that they argued about their children and their disreputable life frequently. Arrie supposedly was accepting of their lifestyle, while George couldn't live with the guilt of the actions of his own sons. Others say that Arrie forced George out after numerous fights about his inability to find work and uselessness to the sons' growing criminal pursuits. After George left, Arrie continued to support and defend the actions of her children.

By 1931, all four of her sons had been locked up in jail. Arrie was living with a man named Arthur W. Dunlop. In the census of that year, she was listed as his wife and living in Tulsa, Oklahoma. There are no records of marriage between the two. This led the Federal Bureau of Investigation (FBI) to later describe her as "a woman of loose morals."

In 1931, Fred Barker was released from prison and joined his former cell mate, Alvin Karpis, to form the Barker-Karpis gang. After a series of daring robberies and other crimes, Fred and Karpis got into a gunfight with Sheriff C. Roy Kelly of West Plains, Missouri. The two gunned down the sheriff and fled the territory out of fear of reprisal from the police in the area. Arrie and Dunlop traveled with them to help as a cover.

Having Arrie around gave the gang a sense of protection of their identities. Checking into boardinghouses or hotels went a lot easier with a middle-aged woman than young toughs who weren't very literate. Karpis once noted that it was a lot easier to pose as a mother with her sons than it would have been for goons and a moll to find a hideout. Ma Barker became known to the gang as "Kate" when the first wanted posters began to offer a $100 reward for the capture of "Old Lady Arrie Barker."

In 1932, Arthur was released from jail and joined the gang. First, they went to Chicago, but running afoul of Al Capone, the gang quickly moved to St. Paul, Minnesota. The gang operated in the open there, as it was given protection by the city's corrupt police chief, Thomas "Big Tom" Brown. The police chief even offered guidance to the up-and-coming gang in helping it to escalate its operations.

Moving from house to house around town and still using Ma Barker as the face for these hideouts worked for a long while. Eventually, however, they were spotted by a local resident. Big Tom tipped off the gang, hearing of its impending arrest. They all quickly made their escape. Barker's lover, Dunlop, was found naked and murdered with a bullet to the head near

Webster, Wisconsin, shortly thereafter. Karpis had apparently thought he had been the tipster.

Fred and Karpis knew that Ma was no longer an asset and sent her away to several hideouts. Some historians say that it was a power struggle, but most think it was simply that Kate was overprotective of her sons. The girls the sons used to bring home did not meet her approval and were often treated poorly by Ma Barker.

After two successful kidnappings of prominent local businessmen, the gang was finally on the run from the FBI thanks to a new method of latent fingerprint identification. Big Tom had been drummed out of the police force in St. Paul. Without his protection, the gang moved back to Chicago.

The Barker-Karpis gang exploded onto the gangster scene of 1930s Chicago with bank robberies and kidnappings. It even teamed up or worked with other notorious criminal underworld figures like Homer Van Meter and John Dillinger. Ma Barker was moved around a lot to keep her away from the gang's activities. Eventually, she was sent to Florida.

On January 8, 1935, Arthur "Doc" Barker was arrested in Chicago. The authorities searched his apartment and found a letter from his mother. This letter invited Arthur to join them on their property in Central Florida. It also described an unnamed lakefront property. There was a map with the letter, but it was still very vague. The only true lead was that Ma mentioned in her letter that Arthur's brother Fred had vowed to kill a local giant alligator named "Old Joe" and had even shot at the giant beast with his Tommy gun.

The FBI flooded Marion County in the heart of Florida after narrowing down the map's location. Agents swarmed the cities of mid-Florida looking for Ma and Fred. It only took a few days for someone to recognize Ma's picture. One informant had even heard machine gun fire around a particular house. He believed that the men must have been shooting at Old Joe out in the waters of Lake Weir. The FBI surrounded the house in Ocklawaha and called for the gang to come out on January 16, 1935.

Karpis and most of the gang had left just a few days ahead of the raid. Only Fred and Ma Barker were in the house. After being ordered to surrender by the agents, Fred opened fire himself from an upstairs window. The gunfight that followed is the stuff of legend. Hours passed, and there are stories of neighbors coming and having a picnic while the FBI continuously poured fire into the house on the lake. When the gunfire finally stopped, the FBI ordered a local handyman to enter the home. Willie Woodbury was given a bulletproof vest and sent into the house while the FBI remained outside. He shouted out to the federal agents that no one was alive in the house.

Both bodies were found in the second-floor front bedroom. Fred had been shot multiple times, but Ma had only been shot once. The FBI claimed she had a Tommy gun in her hand; others at the scene say it was merely on the floor near her body. This is where historians say that her role in the gang was exaggerated to justify her killing and the sheer craziness of the already infamous gunfight.

The rest of the gang and her sons were mostly dead or in prison by the end of the decade. Lloyd Barker was the only one to try to redeem himself after prison and went on to serve as an army cook during World War II. He was killed by his wife in 1949. She was sent to an insane asylum for the crime.

Ma Barker would live on in movies, songs and novels. Old Joe, the giant creature in question, would outlive the gang by a few years. In 1952, Joe was killed by local alligator hunter Vic Skidmore. The foot of the massive beast is still on display at the bar named after him just a few blocks away from where the gunfight occurred. The giant gator's carcass did have

A crowd gathers outside the infamous home of Ma Barker the day after the biggest shootout in FBI history. *St. Petersburg Museum of History.*

Gator Joe's Bar and Grill on Lake Weir is named after the infamous giant gator. *Author's photo.*

numerous old bullet holes in his skin, many from a Tommy gun. He was more than fifteen feet long.

Gator Joe's Bar and Grill is a rarity in Central Florida. Although beach bars are common all along the coast of Florida, Gator Joe's is on the freshwater shores of Lake Weir and in the middle of the state. Complete with a white sandy beach, it is a great place for food and fun on the coast of Lake Weir. The story of the namesake gator and Ma Barker are prominently displayed around the bar.

To view Ma's old house, however, you must take a boat ride or drive a long way around the lake now. The house was recently floated across the lake onto the Carney Island Recreation and Conservation area. There you can still visit it today. The bullet holes are still there from the FBI shootout with Ma Barker.

HAUNTED DISNEY, LAKE BUENA VISTA

*L*ong before the grand opening on October 1, 1971, the land that would become Walt Disney World was just another swamp in the dead center of Florida. In the 1880s, the nearly 2 million acres of land in the area was owned by one man, Hamilton Disston. He drained much of this land for farming. He was the largest single landowner in the United States at the time.

Prior to Disston, the land was long inhabited by Native American tribes of the area. The lands near here were the refuge of most of the Seminoles, who had fled the state's coastal areas trying to avoid the European settlers from the early sixteenth century onward. The cypress, pine and live oak forests and tropical swamplands remained free of European settlement for many years. Some Spanish missionaries reported on visiting the early tribes of this area in their attempts to convert them to Christianity, but not much was written of them.

Much speculation exists as to the name of the area itself. Kissimmee was often thought to be an Indian word naming the river nearby. The word doesn't seem to come from the Seminole tribe, though. The earlier tribes of the area may have used the word, but its meaning is lost. Some thought it might have been an African word, as freed slaves from the Spanish colonies joined the Native American tribes of the area in the late 1720s. The Spanish had abolished slavery in Florida in 1728.

The state alternated between British and Spanish control for more than one hundred years. Finally, when Florida joined the United States, early pioneers started staking out land claims in the central areas of the state. This was most often in Indian-controlled areas. This led to the Seminole Wars in the state.

A recently rediscovered legend may explain the name of this area. The story was relayed to us by Bram Stoker Award–winning author Owl Goingback. He, in turn, had heard the story from a fellow member of the Seminole tribe. According to the story, the Native Americans of the area had heard of the acts of soldiers and early settlers coming to the area. These acts included burning villages and slaughtering the men of the tribes. The women would be raped, among other atrocities. This would have been around the time of the Indian Removal Act in the 1830s.

As settlement after settlement was burned and the Indians were killed or forcibly removed, the stories would come to the local tribes in the swamps. Fearful of enslavement, death or worse, most of the tribes fled the state. Many other tribes stayed behind, tired of running.

When the white soldiers approached one particular tribal village, a lone Indian woman stepped out in front of the village to confront the approaching marauders. There was no word in their language for rape. She wanted to offer herself in exchange for mercy for the rest of the tribe. She struggled with the English words: "Kissy me! Kissy me!" We'd like to say this story has a happy ending, but it is very unlikely. Owl Goingback is pretty sure the marauders thought she had simply been telling them the name of the village or perhaps the bordering river. It was noted down somewhere, as the name is still there today as Kissimmee.

Fifty years later, Hamilton Disston needed to boost the value of his landholdings in Central Florida. Needing the river deeper to allow steamboats to ship his lumber and other goods to the Gulf of Mexico, he dredged the river now called the Kissimmee River. By 1883, his settlement at this location, known as Allendale, had voted to rename its community Kissimmee after the river that was helping them prosper.

In 1894, a deep freeze hit the area and killed much of the citrus crop. When a worse freeze hit in 1895, the booming economy of Kissimmee from the previous years was all but obliterated. Most of the residents left the area in search of work farther south in Florida. The railroad replaced the steamboat shortly thereafter. The town of Kissimmee became a small cattle ranching community. It remained this way well into the 1950s.

The story of Walt Disney World actually begins way back in 1923 on the other coast of the United States. Walter Elias Disney and his brother Roy arrived in California with a cartoon they had made in Kansas City about a little girl in a cartoon world called *Alice's Wonderland*. Walt wanted to use this film as a sort of pilot to sell an idea of "Alice Comedies" to a distributor. M.J. Winkler from New York saw the film and its potential. He hired the brothers to make the series of cartoons. On October 16, 1923, the Disney Brothers Cartoon Studio was born, with the brothers as equal partners. Shortly thereafter, Roy suggested they change the name simply to Walt Disney Studios.

After making the "Alice Comedies" for several years, they decided to pivot into an all-cartoon series. Walt created Oswald the Lucky Rabbit and, within a year, made twenty-six cartoons with the character. Needing to build up his studio to make more cartoons, he approached the distributor for more funding. The distributor had instead hired his own team of animators, many of them Walt's former employees, to make the Oswald cartoons himself. The distributor knew that this would be cheaper than making them through the Disney brothers.

Walt was crushed to discover that in his original contract, he did not own the rights to Oswald. The distributor had sole production rights to the character. This harsh lesson for the young cartoonist became an important one. From that moment on, he saw to it that he owned everything the company ever made.

Having started in Hollywood in the back part of a real estate office, the studio soon moved into the entire building next door. With the Oswald money, the company built its own studio in 1926 on Hyperion Avenue. After the loss of Oswald, Walt had to come up with a new character in order to keep his fledgling studio afloat. Walt and his chief animator, Ub Iwerks, designed a new character that would go on to change the world.

Cartoon star Mickey Mouse's first two films were very unsuccessful, as they were silent. Walt had been unable to find distribution for them thanks to the new "talkie" pictures taking over at the box office. Walt Disney Studios went back to work and created the first fully synchronized sound cartoon, *Steamboat Willie*. It opened at the Colony Theater in New York on November 18, 1928. Mickey Mouse proved to be an instant hit, and the character was cemented into the annals of history.

Walt Disney Studios' cartoons grew ever more popular in the movies. A man in New York reached out to Walt to license the image of Mickey Mouse to put on a set of pencil tablets he was manufacturing at the time. Walt realized that he had a new potential source of income: merchandising. He took the $300 offer. Within a few years, Mickey Mouse dolls, dishes, figurines and hundreds more products all bore the iconic image of the famous mouse. By 1930, Mickey had his first book, as well as a daily newspaper strip.

In 1934, Walt shook up his business model once again to make a full-length feature film that would be completely animated. The intense undertaking took three years to finish, but *Snow White* was released in 1937. It was a huge box office hit and became the highest-grossing film ever at that time. The studio was finally on firmer footing; Walt knew that the shorts would be steady income, but feature films would represent the big profits. He began to work with his studio on several projects, but then World War II broke out.

His next two feature films, *Pinocchio* and *Fantasia*, were considered theatrical masterpieces of both technical innovation and artistry. Sadly, the foreign markets were gone thanks to the world war. Due to the high costs of producing these films, the studio did not make enough on them to justify them financially.

Dumbo followed by *Bambi* were initially made on modest budgets, but the costs spiraled to meet Walt's vision. Some propaganda films made for the State Department helped the company through the lean times, but even after the war, it was difficult for the struggling studio to find footing. Live-action production was seen as a cheaper alternative, and so *Song of the South* and *So Dear to My Heart* were made. Because these were Walt Disney Studios films, some animated segments were included in them.

The year 1950 ushered in a new era for Disney. Its first big completely live-action film, *Treasure Island*, became an instant hit. The studio also returned to classic animation in a big way with *Cinderella* shortly thereafter. The first few Disney Christmas specials also aired on TV to much success. Walt was starting to plan even bigger.

One business opportunity had piqued Walt's interest. Now a father, he had taken his two daughters to various carnivals, circuses and zoos. He felt that most had been a bit on the dodgy side, with scary carnival ride proprietors running borderline dangerous rides. He would sit on the bench and watch his children on the rides, noting their fun but fearing for their safety. He began to envision a place where children and their parents could go and have fun together on the same rides. The place would be clean with extremely friendly service. The seeds of Disneyland popped into his head, and he began to develop the idea.

During this time, Walt Disney got into television as big as he could. In 1954, he began a new project called Disneyland, an anthology series of movies and shows that would run on all three of the major networks and go through six title changes over its twenty-nine years on air. He also began

The Mickey Mouse Club in 1955, making stars out of a group of very talented young Mouseketeers.

Originally planned as an eight-acre place for his employees, their families and himself to go and spend a day together, Walt quickly realized that he would need much more space to implement his plans. He had the Stanford Research Institute conduct a survey for a 100-acre site somewhere outside but near Los Angeles. He needed space to build rivers, waterfalls, mountains, flying elephants and giant teacups. These attractions would be centered on a giant fairytale castle. Oh, he also wanted moon rockets. With Walt being a huge model railroad fan, he insisted the whole property also have a scenic railway. The company found 160 acres right off the interstate in Anaheim that would do nicely.

When the design stage came around, Walt found that he had more questions than answers. How do you make believable wild animals? How are we going to make a paddleboat? How do we make a huge castle? Walt looked to his Hollywood studio staff for answers. They also came up with the plan of five uniquely themed "lands" within the park. It would allow for them to house such a diverse range of rides without breaking an illusion of reality.

Disneyland opened on July 17, 1955. Using his television shows as marketing tools, the park exploded in popularity. Main Street, U.S.A.; Frontierland; Adventureland; Fantasyland; and Tomorrowland had created what would be dubbed a "theme park." Nearly every attraction center in the world built after it would copy its design to some degree. Although opening day was a disaster with high heat, a plumbers' strike and last-minute work being done, the site turned into a huge success.

Walt began to think bigger. He dreamed of a climate-controlled domed city that would house corporations from all over the world. There would be an urban center and a suburban area for living with a green beltway with parks, golf courses and everything a population could want. Electric monorails and people-movers would transport residents and workers all about this amazing city of the future. No more congestion. No more noisy streets. Life would be lived to the fullest.

Walt began to call this city the "Experimental Prototype Community of Tomorrow." Shortly after the opening of Disneyland, Walt began seeking partners and investors in his dream. Soon after the World's Fair in 1964, Walt and his team of "Imagineers" visited Westinghouse Electric to discuss this Community of Tomorrow. Eventually, they would hit up every major technological company they could. The list of companies included such heavyweights as IBM, DuPont, General Electric and more. While no one seemed to understand the project except Walt, everyone wanted to participate, and blind support was offered by most.

Disney had hoped to surprise the world with his project, but he needed real estate. Now looking for places with more than one thousand acres, he sent his people all over the world. St. Louis; Niagara Falls; Washington, D.C.; and even New Jersey were all considered. New York's now abandoned world's fair site was seriously considered, but Walt wanted formable land and yearlong blue skies. It had to be in Florida.

The EPCOT project land acquisition process was akin to a *Chinatown*-style land grab scheme. To obtain the low-cost property in the now mostly cattle ranch–occupied Reed Creek Basin in Osceola County near the Kissimmee River, Disney formed several small real estate companies. They strategically purchased land and tried to hold off on filing the paperwork for as long as legally possible to try to do it all at once.

Secret companies with names like "Latin-American Development," "Ayefour Corporation," "Tomahawk Properties" and "Reedy Creek Ranch Company" managed to buy tons of property throughout the Central Florida region. Most ranchers were happy to sell their mostly worthless swamplands for about $150 per acre. Once word leaked out in the *Orlando Sentinel* that Walt Disney was buying up all the property, prices quickly skyrocketed. Walt had most of the land he needed, so purchases stopped with over twenty-seven thousand acres acquired for EPCOT. Twice the size of Manhattan had been purchased for just over $5 million.

Standing between Walt and his future city were the members of the Florida legislature. Tax brackets, zoning issues and thousands more legal issues would constantly pop up. Building a new city in the middle of a big state was going to be a nigh-impossible task. Walt needed freedom to accomplish his dreams.

Walt made a vague promotional film with concept art and model mockups from his Imagineers. The "Florida Film" showed just how amazing EPCOT would be. One version of the film was shown to the Florida legislature, while a second film with variations was shown to the general public on February 2, 1967. Sadly, Walt never saw it. He passed away in 1966.

His passing slowed the progress of the EPCOT project, but the Florida government gave Disney's company the autonomy it wanted. The Reedy Creek Improvement District was formed of two cities, Bay Lake and Reedy Creek. Reedy Creek would later be renamed Lake Buena Vista. This left Disney in full control over building codes, zoning and planning as long as

Walt Disney with company at press conference in Orlando, Florida. 1965. *State Archives of Florida, Florida Memory.*

7,500 acres would be set aside and never developed. These lands are known as the Wildlife Management Conservation Area. The company purchased more land over the years to develop and nearly always adds more land to the now more than 30,000 acres of what it calls "green space" that will never be developed in and around the resort.

Since the project was to be built on swampland, it took a lot of creative engineering to make it work. A huge mound of dirt was taken from the area that would become the Seven Seas Lagoon. This dirt mound became the basis for the Magic Kingdom. This means that you are technically walking onto the second floor when you enter the park. The first floor is filled with what Walt called "utilidors," or tunnels. This became the ideal way for workers, called "cast members" at Walt Disney World, to move about without being seen.

To be self-sufficient, the city had to build its own energy plants, food complexes, a giant laundry facility and much more to handle the needs of everyone. It even built its own airstrip to fly commuter planes from Orlando directly to Walt Disney World. Grooves were built into the landing strip so the wheels of the plane would musically play the song "It's a Small Word" as you landed.

With Walt dead and Roy planning retirement, the idea for the city began to falter. Instead, the plans were made for a theme park that would far outdo the original Disneyland in Anaheim. The EPCOT City of Tomorrow became known as Project X and was shelved by the company. On October 1, 1971, Walt Disney World was opened to the public to much fanfare. Roy had insisted the park be named after his brother, as he often said, "Everyone knows Ford cars and trucks, but how many know Henry Ford. I want Walt to be remembered."

Roy died just a few months after the opening of the park. EPCOT never quite turned into the domed futuristic city of tomorrow, but the monorails, audio-animatronics and even the WEDway People Mover made it into what would become the greatest theme park in the world.

Now that we've finally gotten the history out of the way, let's talk ghosts. There is a famous rumor that Disney doesn't allow anyone to be declared dead at the park. This is simply not true, as there have been plenty of accidental and natural deaths at the park over the years. With nearly 150,000 visitors per day to the parks and so many hidden secrets, there has to be a dark side of Walt Disney World, doesn't there?

A view of the Haunted Mansion and the *Liberty Belle* from a 1971 postcard. *St. Petersburg Museum of History Archives.*

The most famous ghost in Walt Disney World isn't in the Haunted Mansion; he is in another popular attraction, the Pirates of the Caribbean ride. There is a ghost here named George. Every morning, Disney cast members have to say, "Hi, George," over the loudspeaker system or all kinds of trouble will befall the ride that day.

George was apparently a carpenter on the ride who died during construction. His presence is most often felt in the town-burning scene or just under the bridge with the pirate dangling his foot. The service door near the dog with the keys at the jail is often called "George's Door." It is often found open just before a ride glitch causes a stop.

George also must be told, "Good night, George," over the PA at close. Some guests have scoffed at the legend and paid the price when they get stuck in the attraction for long periods of time with an unexpected breakdown. George apparently didn't take kindly to some of the recent changes to the ride. The ghost likes to pester Johnny Depp's Captain Sparrow animatronics that have been added to the ride with frequent malfunctions.

Another ghost has been sighted here of a young woman who may have died when a boat slipped the tracks at the end of the drop. She is seen wet and standing over the water near the big pirate ship battle just after the drop. One guest thought she was a new addition to the ride and tried to snap her picture. All he got was a stringy line of light in the image on his phone. Her story has not been able to be verified. Neither has George's, for that matter. Thanks to these two ghosts, however, Pirates of the Caribbean remains the most haunted ride at the park.

There are more stories of ghosts all over the Magic Kingdom. A disembodied hand is seen reaching out of a cast member door near the Little Mermaid's grotto. The hand looks like it belongs to one of the cast members from the long-destroyed 20,000 Leagues Under the Sea attraction. An interesting fact about that attraction is that at one point, the Walt Disney Company owned the third-largest submarine fleet in the world thanks to the Nautilus submarines from that ride at WDW and Disneyland. Only the United States and Russia owned more submersible watercraft.

A ghostly hanged man is often seen in the Peter Pan's Adventure ride. Just after flying through the window of the Darlings' house on the ride, guests frequently report seeing the man dangling behind them. There are no reports of a suicide here, but so many sightings of this ghost lead one to consider that it is more than just urban legend.

Tom Sawyer Island was designed by Imagineers, but Walt was unhappy with their designs. He took the plans home and completed the redesign overnight. For years, many guests going through the tunnels and caves of the attraction have reported shadow people and quickly moving shapes in the dark corridors on the island. Many more visitors just say the whole island simply unnerves them.

Of course, there are 999 happy haunts in the Haunted Mansion. In truth, though, there may be a few more. A man with a cane is often seen walking outside and riding the ride late at night. When cast members approach to tell him that the park is closing, he simply vanishes out of sight.

One often-rumored spirit in the mansion is that of a little boy. Now there is a famous ghost of a little boy in the Haunted Mansion at Disneyland who cries looking for his mother. This boy in the WDW Haunted Mansion, however, seems to be happy as can be riding the Doombuggies endlessly. There are several photos circulating on the Internet reportedly showing this particular ghost. Cast members mostly believe that this one is just a modern urban legend.

The biggest mystery at the Haunted Mansion is the dust. Nearly two hundred tons of dust have to be imported every year to give the attraction the appropriate scary cobweb-covered and dusty look inside. The cast does not clean the ride, but there are some areas for maintenance that do require some modest cleaning. The real question, then, is where does all the dust go? Walt Disney World must keep importing more and more dust nearly every day to keep up the creepy atmosphere.

The Walt Disney Company built more parks over the years. The first was EPCOT, which was a pale shadow of Walt's dream community and mostly built as a way to prevent overcrowding at the Magic Kingdom. Disney MGM Studios, later renamed Disney's Hollywood Studios, joined next. Disney's Animal Kingdom also arrived a short while later. Numerous resorts and side attractions have come and gone over the years. Pleasure Island and Disney Village became Downtown Disney and now Disney Springs. More and more changes are ongoing as of this writing.

The new parks have ghostly legends of their own. Spaceship Earth in EPCOT is known for two children, a boy and a girl, who are often seen playing and riding together but disappearing before it's time to get off the ride or when approached. Impressions de France is often said to have a shadowy figure still sitting in the theater after it is closed. When cast members approach, the shadow disappears.

The Tower of Terror at Disney Hollywood Studios is haunted by a former "Bellhop" cast member who reportedly died during his shift in the early days of the attraction. He is often seen on the ride's final run each evening on the infamous Platform D. Lights flicker and the ride freezes in place when he appears. He is so famous that ghost hunters often ask to participate in "the final ride" each evening hoping to catch a glimpse of the bellhop ghost.

The saddest ghost of all is the legacy of Disney's Community of Tomorrow. No one will ever live there. No corporations will ever house their world headquarters there. You can, however, enjoy its aesthetic in every inch of the Walt Disney World Resort. The theme park burrows itself into our dreams, and millions upon millions of visitors go there as often as possible to see even a glimpse of Walt's vision. Walt liked to say, "It all started with a mouse." It really all started with one man's dream.

MONSTERS AND MURDERS IN THE GREEN SWAMP, LAKELAND

*L*ook at any map of Florida and you will see a very large block in the middle of the state with no major roads. The largest area stretches from Lakeland to the north beyond Leesburg. This empty area once saw rival railroads trying to reach Tampa Bay. It once housed numerous little towns and homesteads trying to make their way in the early Florida land booms. Now, from the passage of time, the swamp is reclaiming the last vestiges of man's attempts to colonize the area. The state now controls it and calls it the Green Swamp Wilderness Preserve.

The Green Swamp in Florida is sometimes nicknamed "Emerald Hell." Most of the year, it is hot and full of mosquitoes and other bugs. This swampy land covers more than 560,000 acres of wetlands, surrounded by ridgelines that help drain the rainwater. This rainwater creates the headwaters of no fewer than four major rivers: the Withlacoochee, Ocklawaha, Hillsborough and Peace Rivers. This area also helps to replenish the primary source of drinking water for almost all of Florida, the aquifer system. In 1974, Florida designated a large portion of the Green Swamp region as an "Area of Critical State Concern."

The green swamp is so large that it includes numerous abandoned ghost towns, rail lines, ranches and more scattered throughout the dense twists of vines and trees. It is easy to see why so many legends and stories circulate among the hunters, hikers and explorers who love Emerald Hell.

The swamp has been home to human life for more than eight thousand years. The Paleo Indians, one of Florida's earliest inhabitants, left traces in the heart of the swamp. They were followed by later Native American tribes and then early European pioneers. These last immigrants would carve

Cabin at the edge of Green Swamp in Lake County, Florida. 189-. *State Archives of Florida, Florida Memory.*

out ranches and small towns and would come into frequent conflict with the animals of the area, including bears, panthers, boars and wolves. The inevitable conflicts with the Native American tribes also escalated, and the Seminole Wars were fought throughout some of the Green Swamp.

The settlement boom collapsed when the railroads moved toward the coasts. The final nail in the coffin would be when the Great Depression hit. What few jobs remained in the few towns in the settlements and towns dried up. The swamp began to reclaim itself.

The Native Americans of the area talked of the Wild Man of the Swamp, who roamed through the heart of this area. The settlers talked of great bears that walked like a man. They would often harass their cattle. Some would talk of the terrible smell of death and decay that heralded the appearance of these great hairy beasts. It is this smell that gave them the nickname that still sticks with them to this day: the Skunk Ape.

As Florida's Sasquatch or Bigfoot type of cryptozoological animal, it is still widely reported in this preserve. Hunters in the area discuss sightings almost as frequently as tales of monster bucks, wild turkeys or wild boars they've seen. Most think of them as harmless but certainly not a myth. What most do not know is that one was at one point a murder suspect.

In May 1918, a couple were found dead at their homestead deep in the Green Swamp. Isham and Sarah Stewart had been murdered in their sleep,

The Florida Skunk Ape. *Illustration by Kari Schultz.*

and due to their remote location, the bodies had not been discovered for at least a week. They were only found due to the large number of vultures covering their cabin. Rumors began to fly of a large animal that mauled them, as their bodies were horribly mutilated. Some suspected that the Green Swamp Skunk Ape had turned violent.

The coroner quite quickly realized that things were different. The couple had been murdered with an axe. A quick investigation revealed that there were rumors in town that Isham had recently withdrawn all his money from the bank and had taken it to their homestead. Those rumors had reached Josh Browning, the grandson of Sarah and Isham.

Josh knew where their cabin was and got his friend John Tucker to accompany him. In the dark of night, they came up to the cabin and viciously murdered the couple in their sleep. Both perpetrators were caught a short while later and, after a trial, were sentenced to twenty years in prison each. Even with their conviction, many stories still circulated that it was the Skunk Ape that did it.

Years later, in 1975, near the Devil's Creek Swamp, one of the many sloughs in the Green Swamp, the legend of the monster that walks this Emerald Hell once again reared its ugly head. Burglary reports flooded in from three counties around the Green Swamp. Most of these involved strange items being stolen, including cookies and cereal from a mobile home. Someone saw a strange beast of a man clubbing an armadillo with some crude weapon and dragging it into the grassy edge of the Devil's Creek Swamp.

Police sent dogs to track the suspect on several occasions, but they quickly lost the scent in the deep swamp. They did find parts of a cooked armadillo. They began to realize this was no Skunk Ape, but most likely just some sort of wild man living on the edge of society.

On May 17, the police mounted a large manhunt into the swamp. After firing a few warning shots when they got close, they captured the "Green Swamp Wild Man." He was a sailor named Hu Tu-Mei. He had left his wife, four sons and three daughters when he sailed from his home in Taipei, Taiwan. He had caused a violent outburst on a freighter in Tampa and was in a fight with other sailors onboard. He was taken to a Tampa Hospital, and from there he disappeared.

Somehow, he had walked deep into the Green Swamp and lived in the wild for nearly a year. Hunters and hikers lost for only a few days in the swamp come out nearly mad and babbling wrecks. Hu had lived out there for a long time. He had cooked the corn the hunters had left for turkeys and deer near hunting blinds. He had fashioned an aluminum pole with an old railroad spike on the end to catch the armadillos that he thought were little pigs that nobody wanted.

He was brought to the Sumter County Jail and charged with theft. He refused to leave his cell and bowed deeply every time someone came in to check on him. A Taiwanese interpreter was brought in, and they learned that Hu feared for his life and felt these officers were going to kill him. He

Photo of the Stewart Homestead as it stands today in the Green Swamp. *David Sidotti, founder of the Independent Sasquatch Research Team.*

wanted to kill himself rather than face whatever punishment they had in store for him. He was searching for anything he could hurt himself with, and arrangements were made to fly him back to Taiwan.

Sadly, a few days later, Hu looped his belt through the bars in his cell and strangled himself. The sheriff said, "Hu Tu-Mei was alone and frightened in a strange land." He also felt that now the stories of a large monster with huge feet and a foul odor would fall away. He was very wrong. To this day, there are sightings of the Florida Skunk Ape, and they are becoming more frequent. Researchers mount trips into the Green Swamp at known hotspots. Rangers even have reports of incidents with things they can't easily explain.

David Sidoti and the Independent Sasquatch Research Team have spent years tracking sightings of the Skunk Ape all over Florida—from the ones down in the Everglades and those in the Ocala National Forest, which we covered in *Eerie Florida*, to the ones near the panhandle and even southern Georgia. David and his team have traveled a great portion of the Green Swamp and have found plenty of eyewitness accounts to know that there is almost certainly something to the stories. Some sightings even occur at the old Stewart Homestead, which still stands after more than one hundred years and several major hurricanes, including 2017's Irma.

Visitors to the site of the old homestead can even visit the graves of Sarah and Isham Stewart, just a short distance from their old cabin, deep in the woods. Make sure to keep an eye out for large, hairy observers just out of sight in the tree line.

The state continues to buy land for the preserve to help with water management for the increasing demands of Florida's continuing population boom. The Green Swamp grows, and its heart gets darker and harder to reach. It is an ominous place filled with abandoned settlements, ghost towns, Indian mounds and old rail lines. It is a great place for hiking, exploring and, of course, hunting. Almost anything could be out there.

ROSEWOOD MASSACRE, SUMNER

Rosewood was a small town just a short distance from Cedar Key on the Gulf Coast of Florida, about halfway between Tampa and Tallahassee. Though still legally an unincorporated community in Levy County, little remains of what was once a prosperous community except for some abandoned businesses, a cemetery and a historical marker telling the chilling tale of how the town was destroyed by racial violence in 1923.

Like most of Florida, Rosewood was predominately settled in the 1890s shortly after the Civil War. The town was named for the red cedar wood that populated the area. Logging operations drew workers and their families. Both black and white families flowed into the town, and several pencil mills set up shop in the town. But by 1890, deforestation had caused the mills to close, and the town began to fragment. Most of the white population moved to the neighboring town of Sumner less than a mile away, as it was friendly to whites. Rosewood became a predominantly black city.

With more than three hundred people and a few prominent black families, the town prospered, most notably the Goins family, who brought in the turpentine industry. The Goins brothers were among some of the most prominent landowners in the state. Although they lived in Gainesville, their business investments in turpentine and lumber were still mostly in the areas around Cedar Key, including Rosewood.

By the early 1920s, the entire town had become very close, and most inhabitants were related to one another, at least distantly, since so few moved in or out of the area. While the turpentine industry would fade in the coming decade, it was still prosperous at this time. Trade with the nearby towns of Cedar Key and Sumner from Rosewood oyster beds and citrus farms kept the town afloat.

Relations with the neighboring towns degraded as a series of incidents increased racial tensions. In 1922, a white schoolteacher from nearby Perry was murdered. Many claimed that the unknown assailant was black. With no real witnesses, the case went unsolved—but many blamed a known criminal named Jesse Hunter from Rosewood.

On New Year's Eve 1922, the Ku Klux Klan held a rally in Gainesville. At the Klan rally, someone said their wife had been sexually assaulted by a black man at her home in Cedar Key. It did not take long for word to spread. Racial tensions had stretched to the breaking point.

On January 1, 1923, a group of white men acting on this rumor went to Rosewood. The men believed that the woman, Fanny Taylor, had been beaten up by the recently escaped convict Jesse Hunter. Since Hunter was originally from there, they assumed he would be hiding in Rosewood.

In their search for Jesse Hunter, the men quickly learned the names of two of his former friends, Aaron Carrier and Sam Carter. Feeling they must be accomplices of the escaped Hunter, the mob of men swarmed the town. Carrier was quickly captured. The white men looped a rope around his neck and dragged him behind a car for a great distance. A local sheriff named Walker put a stop to it just in time to save the boy. Sam Carter was also caught by the mob. Before the sheriff could act in his case, Carter was lynched.

The mob was broken up by Sheriff Walker, but members felt that Sylvester Carrier, a cousin of Aaron's, must be involved and may even be harboring Jesse Hunter. They reorganized, and more white men joined the pack as they prepared to return to Rosewood as soon as possible.

The community of Rosewood was reeling from the violence. They knew more could be coming, so many families fled into the nearby woods and swamps. Most of the men in the town prepared their homes for defense for the inevitable attack. They did not have long to wait.

On January 4, 1923, a group of nearly thirty men surrounded the home of Sylvester Carrier. Sarah Carrier, Sylvester's mother, came to the front porch to confront the men outside her house. As she stepped out, she was shot and killed. Sylvester returned fire. Before the battle was over, the young man killed two of the mob and wounded four others before being shot himself. The rest of the Carrier family fled into the swamps, joining many of the Rosewood refugees.

Deliberate burning of an African American home in Rosewood, Florida. 1923. *State Archives of Florida, Florida Memory.*

As the sun rose on January 5, the white mob was nearing two hundred men. Most came because they'd heard a black man had killed two white men. The men swarmed the town, slaughtering animals, burning buildings and attacking anyone who got in their way. By the end of the day, six more black men had been killed by the angry mob. Two of the white men who had attacked the town had been killed by Rosewood citizens who had refused to flee their homes.

Most of the refugees at this point had fled to Gainesville or farther north. Several families were assisted in their escape by two local train conductors, brothers John and William Bryce. The two had traded with the people of Rosewood regularly and came to help. The mob had burned the town to the ground—the only two buildings remaining were the general store and one house. These were owned by John Wright, a white man who also helped hide several survivors in the store.

Fannie Taylor's story of rape began to unravel. Several of her family's servants mentioned a frequent visitor, John Bradley, who worked for the railroad. It seemed Bradley liked to visit Mrs. Taylor while her husband

Ruins of a burned African American home in Rosewood. 1923. *State Archives of Florida, Florida Memory.*

was away at work. Her beating had been from this man, her secret lover. It seemed apparent that she had made up the story of rape by a mysterious black man to hide her infidelity.

The newspapers had a field day with this "race war" in Rosewood, and accounts are many and varied. Some said that as many as thirty whites lay dead. Others listed black fugitives and the Fannie Taylor rape story as a justifiable instigation. The *Tampa Tribune* was a lone dissenter, calling the action "a foul and lasting blot on the people of Levy County."

Governor Cary Hardee appointed a grand jury and a special prosecuting attorney to investigate the violence. By the end of February 1923, the all-white grand jury had convened. More than two dozen witnesses—of whom only eight were black—came forward to discuss the attacks. The jury found "insufficient evidence" to prosecute anyone involved.

With early tourism to the state threatened, pressure mounted for the stories to disappear. The official death count was eight people: six black and two white. Most historians disagree with the official reports. Many survivors, interviewed after the massacre, claimed that at least twenty-five to thirty black residents had been killed and that the newspapers also underreported the number of white deaths. There were reports of a mass grave, and several of the young survivors spoke in their later years of walking across many dead bodies.

A strange culture of silence began. Rosewood was completely destroyed and abandoned. Most of the survivors started over in new towns. Many never mentioned their origins for fear of reprisals. Others simply didn't want their own children to know of the horrors that occurred. It wouldn't be until the 1980s that the story resurfaced.

By 1993, law firms were suing the State of Florida for failing to protect the survivors and their families. This lawsuit was filed on behalf of many survivors who were just beginning to tell their tales so many years later. After lengthy discussions and proposals, the Rosewood Compensation Bill passed the legislature and was signed by Governor Lawton Chiles in 1994. Those who could prove they were descended from families of Rosewood or were among the few living survivors were entitled to share in a pool of money from the state. A Rosewood Family Scholarship Fund was also established for descendants and then opened for all minorities.

Several books and a 1997 feature film directed by John Singleton brought the story back from the depths of history. In 2004, Rosewood was declared a Florida Heritage Landmark, and a historical marker was placed. In Daytona Beach on the far side of the state, there is a permanent display in the library at Bethune-Cookman University. The artifacts and documents occasionally tour to educate the world about the attacks.

If you travel State Road 24 toward the quiet beach town of Cedar Key, you'll pass the marker where once stood Rosewood. Take a moment to help preserve the memory of the horrors that occurred.

CRYSTAL RIVER MOUNDS, CRYSTAL RIVER

While Floridians love to talk about St. Augustine being the most continuously inhabited city in America, having just celebrated its 450th birthday a few years ago, there is one site on the opposite coast that was occupied for a much longer span. For at least 1,600 years, Native Americans occupied a complex of mounds dating back to 200 BC in Crystal River. The site has been studied for nearly one hundred years, but much of its history and even its intended purpose still remains a mystery.

As with many Native American sites in Florida, there are shell middens here. Middens are usually directly associated with villages and other sites of some continuous habitation by the early inhabitants of the Florida peninsula. As the Native Americans would eat oysters, deer and other game food, they would deposit their shells and bones in a pile, similar in manner to our modern-day landfills. These piles would be layered with dirt and rise in pyramid-like mounds. Many of these would reach great height and scope, containing millions and millions of shells.

The mound complex at the mouth of the Crystal River is from pre-contact Native Americans. Sadly, this means there are no written records of the tribe in this area. Their tribal name is lost to history. Historians are still debating the main purpose of the site to this day.

It appears that the earliest mounds in the area were for burial purposes. Many of the artifacts found near bodies buried here include rare copper artifacts. Copper is not local to Florida. This would appear to show that there

The stele monument at the Crystal River Archaeological State Park aligns with the mounds. Note the faded carving of a human face. *Author's photo.*

The view from the Temple Mound in Crystal River. *Author's photo.*

was a large trade network throughout the early North American continent among the early inhabitants.

There are several burial mounds throughout the complex. There are also many shell middens here. The most striking mounds at this location are the two great platform mounds. These giant hills were built at different periods during the site's 1,600 years of habitation.

The large mound right at the edge of the Crystal River is often called the Temple Mound. It is an impressive site rising high over the flat, surrounding Florida landscape. The mound must have been even more impressive when it was built about 1,400 years ago, as it would have been about four times as large as it is now. A large portion of the Temple Mound was carried away and used as road fill before the site became protected. The mound is thought by archaeologists to be a site of religious ceremonies.

A second large mound on the other side of the complex is also thought to be ceremonial in nature. The second mound is not as high but stretches farther along the far side of the complex. It contains what some archaeologists believe to be a staging area. This would have been for the chieftain or shaman to prepare before rising to the top of the mound for the gathered masses on the other side. Historians admit this is all speculative. The theory does seem sound and would echo that of the Mayan and Aztec cultures from Central and South America.

Some prehistory experts believe that the large mounds were not ceremonial but may have been a home for important people in the tribe. Most of the artifacts recovered from various archaeological digs at the site

are still available to be viewed at the cultural center located on the site. While still undergoing further study, theories on the site and its peoples vary to this day.

Research shows that they were a highly adaptive culture and used every resource available. Stone tools, shell tools, tortoise shells and arrowheads are all available for viewing and show how inventive the people here were. Items made of copper and galena, which must have been traded by the Indians as far away as the Ohio River Valley, are examples of the vast trade system of which they must have been a part. Pottery and other artifacts on display allow visitors to view artifacts from the multiple eras of inhabitation of the Crystal River complex.

There are two very large rock structures here. These are called stele. Stele No. 1 appears to have the remains of a very primitive carved face with long hair. Stele No. 2 is located directly in front of the Temple Mound. No one is truly sure what these stones signify or even why they are located where they are within the complex.

Archaeologists and historians have theories about these ancient stones as well. Many believe that the complex of mounds and the stele are some attempt at an early astronomical calendar. Some believe they may have been simply a ceremonial or memorial marker. A third stele is marked at the site, but most believe it was added at a much later date than the others.

The biggest question at the Crystal River mound complex considers what happened to the culture that was here. No European ever met up with these Native Americans, as they had mostly disappeared by about AD 1000. Although there are some signs of habitation as late as AD 1400, it still predates the early explorers by some time. No tribe claims a descent from these people. So why did they leave?

Legends rise up here, as some say the stele is the answer. There is a tale of a lone warrior who faced a great earth spirit near the temple mound. As the great spirit made of earth and mud rose from the Crystal River, the shaman blessed the warrior to battle it. The battle lasted for days, as the people fled the complex and spread out among the other tribes of Florida. The stele is said to hold the warrior's visage as he died so that his people might escape.

The Crystal River Archaeological State Park today is a fun place to picnic, barbecue and just watch for wildlife. The park also holds "Moon Over the Mounds" events nearly every full moon, with a sunset tour led by historians. At these events, the mounds are lit by torches, and the cultural center is filled with extra exhibits and historians with even more tales to tell. It is a great place to visit and learn a piece of the distant past of Florida that remains mostly a mystery.

THE TRAGEDIES OF OAK HURST, OCALA

Beatrice Marean wrote a novel called *The Tragedies of Oak Hurst* about the fictional town of Magnolia Centre. In the preface, the author admitted that the plot is based "largely on fact" and "the majority of the characters are from real life." She also admitted to embellishing the real stories with "the bright threads of romance into the somber warp of truth." The book was released to much acclaim.

Shortly after the book was published in 1891, a scandal began in Ocala, Florida. Prominent locals in the city began to recognize themselves in the pages of that book. Stories circulated that local families tried to buy up all available copies. Legend states that the author and her husband were discovered and forced from the town. Magnolia Centre was obviously Ocala.

The author was really Dr. Rene R. Snowden, the wife of a famous Ocala druggist and a fine chemist in her own right. She had completed the novel in 1890 and released it under the pseudonym of Beatrice Marean to keep it from interfering with her work at the chemical laboratory she managed. The reason for their sudden move from Ocala had nothing to do with the scandal the book caused, but rather the fact that she and her husband had discovered phosphate in Dunnellon and planned on investing heavily in the area.

The legend Snowden wrote about was of Oak Hurst Plantation, a real place in Ocala. According to the stories of the location, the owner and his wife went riding one day. She fell from her horse when a strange white mare bolted in front of them. She died instantly from the fall, and the white horse vanished; the owner committed suicide shortly after returning home.

The Oakhurst Plantation's spectral horse appears to warn the town of Ocala of impending disasters. *Illustration by Kari Schultz.*

For years after, the strange white horse would race up to the front of the plantation house and snort loudly. When a crowd would gather to observe the horse, it would mysteriously disappear. Shortly after the strange equine visitation, a tragic event would befall the town or a prominent figure in the city would die. The story of the white mare was widely known, as it was famously spotted the day before the burning of downtown Ocala in 1883.

In the book, a bride is shot while riding her white horse and dies in her husband's arms. He then shoots himself. Years pass, and a doctor arrives and buys the house with the help of a money lender. The money lender seizes the property but is killed, and the doctor must prove his innocence.

The horse returns again and again as body after body, tragedy after tragedy, pile up. The book is quite extensive and even includes a famous train wreck heralded by the appearance of the white horse. The true murderer is revealed at the end and life returns to normal at Oak Hurst, but the legendary horse still rides in one last time.

In the early 1980s, the last remains of Oak Hurst Plantation's frame were removed, and the city sold the land. A nursing home called Oakhurst Manor

The Oak Hurst Retirement Home now resides on the grounds of the old Oakhurst Plantation. *Author's photo.*

and an apartment complex are all that remain on Lake Weir Avenue, where the Oak Hurst Plantation once stood.

The big white horse is still seen sometimes by residents of the apartments, as well as the nursing home staff. One nurse, who wished to remain anonymous, told us that they know when someone at the home is about to fall ill or die, for the staff still hears the hoof beats outside to this very day.

The Snowdens' investment in the phosphate mines of Dunnellon paid off, and it put that small town on the map. The book sales and acclaim were nice, but the money from the phosphate industry became the family trade.

Today, *The Tragedies of Oak Hurst*, now more than a century old, is extremely hard to get hold of. The legend, however, lives on.

THE BROOKSVILLE RAID, BROOKSVILLE

*I*n mid-January each year, the largest group of Civil War reenactors in Florida gathers together to replay the infamous Brooksville Raid. Cannons and cavalry charges echo across the modern-day battlefield. Battle lines form, and the soldiers begin their barrage of rifle fire as smoke fills the air. It is an amazing sight and a must-see for Central Florida. The reenactors go to extreme lengths to ensure historical accuracy in their battle and dress. In truth, this amazing modern tableau of the Civil War has very little to do with the historical accuracy of the event itself.

As the Civil War raged on, Hernando County on Florida's Gulf Coast played a vital role as a great resource center for the Confederacy. The plantations of the area provided salt, cattle and cotton. The bulk of these crops was shipped out via the local costal community wharf in the area of modern-day Bayport, Florida.

Being located in the middle of Florida, no large Confederate force was left to defend the region. The need for troops in the battles to the north was far greater. The defense of the county was left to a "home guard." This volunteer force was composed of a few regular soldiers bolstered by old men and young boys from the nearby communities. It was a force of about sixty men all told. These men were led by a preacher named Captain Leroy Lesley, who had served in the United States Army during the Seminole Indian Wars.

This ragtag militia's primary purpose was usually guarding cattle drives to the north. The men also would help organize the defense of blockade

The cannons of the Union army line the field of the Brooksville Raid in 2018. *Author's photo.*

runners as they loaded and delivered cargo to and from the wharf. The Union navy dominated the Gulf Coast. These blockade runners were an essential lifeline to get the supplies out of Hernando County and to the rest of the Confederacy.

As the war raged on, especially in the later years, the once vital resource center was now all but bankrupt. Many in the area were starving. Florida had two bad crop years in a row from 1863 to 1864. Most of the cattle had been sent north for the war effort, primarily to Gainesville. The residents of the area were in dire straits.

Union forces decided to organize a joint operation with their army and navy to deal a crippling blow to the Confederate export centers along the Gulf Coast. A fighting force was formed that included men from the Second Florida Cavalry and a squad of mostly African American "Buffalo Soldiers." They left the Union fort in Tampa via boat and headed to Anclote Key, north of Tampa Bay, in early July 1864.

The unit of just over two hundred men made landfall on July 7 and set out for Brooksville on foot. They were ordered to sack the town and return to the Gulf. The march was scheduled to take them seven days and end at the Bayport Wharf. Navy forces would meet them there and transport them back to Tampa. By the next morning, plans were already changing.

Union forces discovered a campfire ahead of them to the north from their camp on the morning of July 8. The troops broke camp and formed ranks to march. An advance guard was sent ahead to investigate the smoke. The advance guard consisted of ten men under the command of Captain Henry Crane. These men overcame a small group of Confederate home guard skirmishers in a short exchange of rifle fire along a road. The brief fight led to a slight wounding of one Union soldier in the largely bloodless battle. Seven Confederates were captured, as were nine horses.

The Union forces quickly realized that their deadline to rendezvous with the navy forces in Bayport in just a few days was already in jeopardy. Between the skirmish and the dense swampy terrain, they were already moving far too slowly.

Confederate captain Lesley's platoon of home guard began to harass the Union soldiers in a series of hit-and-run ambushes. Outnumbered three to one, the home guard was relentless. They continued to engage the Union forces as they tried to plod their way to Brooksville. At some point, the Union forces decided to spare Brooksville to keep up with their timetable. They turned and made their way directly toward Bayport. At least four plantations in the area were burned and looted on the way.

The Confederate camp at the Brooksville Raid. *Author's photo.*

By July 13, the Union force had made its way to Bayport and boarded the waiting ships with their pillaged cotton, cattle and other goods from all over Hernando County. During their raids, they had burned the home of Captain Lesley himself. The citizens of the area were shaken to the core, and the damage was extensive.

Throughout the cat-and-mouse game of skirmishes from the Confederates' campaign to slow the Union, there was only one casualty. One lone Union solider who had been taken as a prisoner of war had been killed by Lesley. There were several wounded on both sides, although most wounds were superficial. One of the wounded was Captain Lesley's own son, John T. Lesley, who had been accidentally shot by his own father when he mistook him for a Union soldier on one dark evening of the chase.

The true toll on the county was that many fled and never returned. It would take several years, well after the end of the war, before the area would return to even some semblance of normalcy. To this day, the area is growing much slower than the areas around it, although the pace is quickening thanks to Florida's ever-increasing population.

Every year, more than 1,500 reenactors come to the Sand Hill Scout Reservation. The spectators flood "Sutlers' Row" to find souvenirs, turkey legs or homemade root beer before setting up their lawn chairs along the battlefield. The cannons roar and the horses charge. The smoke fills the old field. You can't help but be drawn into the history.

Just remember that the actual history of the battle itself was extremely different. It is considered a Confederate victory by the locals, where Captain Lesley and his outnumbered troops saved Brooksville and routed the Union forces to the sea. In truth, the city took years to recover as everyone fled the approach of the Union soldiers, and the breadbasket of Florida never again fed the Confederacy.

THE WONDERHOUSE, BARTOW

The city of Bartow lies nestled nearly in the middle of the Florida peninsula. It was founded in 1851 as the state was beginning to see settlements south of Gainesville. The Seminole Wars had ended, but the land was treacherous and the heat and humidity nearly intolerable. The remaining Seminole tribe members who had refused to go to Oklahoma were generally peaceful, but settlers were very afraid of them. The large port cities like Tampa drew most of the population of early settlers, so Bartow remained a small town.

Shortly after the Civil War, the town was named after the first Confederate officer to die in the war, Francis S. Bartow. The first courthouse, high school and churches were built. The city grew quickly in the 1880s, and by the start of the twentieth century, it was the third-most populous city in Central Florida. This pace did not keep up—as the rest of the state boomed, Bartow slowed down. Despite being the home of the largest phosphate industry in the United States, the beaches and sun were drawing people away from the heart of the state.

In 1925, a contractor from Pittsburgh named Conrad Shuck was told that he had little time left to live. His life of dealing with stone quarries was catching up with him. His doctors told him that if he was lucky, he would last the year. Having a substantial sum of money from his building days, he looked for a place to take his family to live his final days in peace.

Many told Shuck that Florida had this amazing restorative atmosphere that might extend his days a little. He decided to head to the Sunshine State and build a dream home for his family. His hope was that they could live on in luxury without him.

Knowing of the phosphate mines near Bartow, Shuck figured that the area had plenty of quarries and the materials he would need to build the family mansion he had envisioned. His wife and their nine children all came with him to the town of Bartow. Within the year, construction had begun on Shuck's dream.

The land he had purchased was just like most of the rest of Florida and had a foundation of limestone bedrock. Shuck used this to dig out a solid foundation and a basement. The house would be four stories, with two above ground and two below. Basements are an extreme rarity in Florida. The house would be built with a central cross theme and porches on all four sides of every story. This would allow for windows to be opened on the sides to allow for a cross breeze to ease the Florida heat. Plans were forming, but no blueprints were made.

With good wood hard to come by, Shuck lucked into a large number of steel rail lines from a railroad company that wanted to be rid of them. Shuck used these iron rails to reinforce the concrete and stone walls of his house. He imported tile, glass and colored stones to inlay into the concrete to give the house impressive color and details mostly unheard of at the time of its construction.

The porches were built with hollow columns of concrete. These would gather rainwater and provide a sort of cooling system for the house. This would also supply water to the planters built into the concrete around the house. Faucets built into the columns would allow the planters to be watered. These plants surrounded the porches, giving the house a look of greenery growing out of it. It gained the nickname the "Breeder House."

Shuck filled the house with marvelous oddities of construction. A sunken bathtub was most often remarked about. A prism-mounted fireplace with a mirror system for enhanced lighting was another. One ingenious device was built by one of his sons: a Lazy Susan cabinet turntable in the kitchen area. It would spin to allow access from nearly 360 degrees with sliding doors. The living room ceiling was designed to have removable panels so that each one could be painted with different designs and removed to redecorate for various holidays.

A third-floor porch had a large fish pond that was filled with koi. Deep into the foundation, there was a pump room for all the water. A piping system was built to the terraced pool. The concrete bridges with interlaced tile and glass looked down onto the pool with stocked fish. The pump kept

The Wonderhouse from a 1939 advertisement. *St. Petersburg Museum of History.*

the water fresh. Between this and many other ingenious and unorthodox construction techniques, it also was sometimes called the "House of a Thousand Marvels."

As the Great Depression hit the nation, hard times also hit the Shuck family. They had still yet to finish the house and lived across the way. Neighbors convinced them to open the house for tours to help them weather the financial disaster. A small fee would get you access to tour what was finally called "the Wonderhouse."

The house's fame spread. Soon it was featured in one of the famous *Ripley's Believe It or Not!* cartoons of the day. Tourism boomed in Florida in the '30s and '40s. The Wonderhouse was featured prominently in many state roadmaps and postcards of the era.

Conrad Shuck long outlived his one-year prognosis of 1925. The hard work on the house, with his children helping, had been the right tonic for him. He lived more than forty more years. He did not die until 1971. The odd thing is the Shuck family never actually lived in the Wonderhouse. They instead lived across the way in their own home. They sold the Wonderhouse in 1964 to the DuCharme family, who completed the construction.

The house changed hands again and again, with new owners making changes and sometimes covering up the creativity of Shuck and his family.

The view of the Wonderhouse as it is being currently renovated. *Author's photo.*

At several points, the property was actually empty and began to fall into disrepair. Those not knowing the history of the house began to form dark legends and spooky tales about the mysterious, abandoned building. Tales of hauntings and other ghoulish stories began to circulate.

In 2015, the property went to auction, and a family bought the Wonderhouse. The new owners have begun to work on the property and are attempting to restore it to some semblance of its original state. While eventually they intend to reopen it to the public in some form, they have quite a lot of work ahead of them. We were given a rare glance into some of the work they are doing and saw some of the marvels they have restored. I can assure you that the wait will be well worth it. You can view their progress on the Wonderhouse Facebook page or at www.wonderhousebartow.com.

We would like to remind readers that the Wonderhouse is their private residence. Trespassing is strictly forbidden! The house is nearly one hundred years old and still being restored. The couple are working on it daily, but it will take time before it reopens. Thankfully, you can still walk by the edge of the property; look at this amazing marvel of a home, surrounded by beautiful mossy trees; and still see the intricate tile and glass designs worked into the concrete by a man who at one point only had one year to live.

THE GHOSTS OF THE CUBAN CLUB, TAMPA

T he Cuban Club in Ybor City was also known as El Circulo Cubano de Tampa. It was built in 1917 after the original building burned down the previous year. It was a gathering place for Cuban immigrants in Ybor City who were the primary workforce of Tampa's booming cigar industry. This replacement building would be made of brick and stone to replace the wooden building that had burned so quickly in 1916.

The original club had been established in 1902. It was a mutual aid society among the Cuban immigrants of Tampa's booming cigar factories to help pool their resources and talents. It was a great place to mingle with fellow Cuban expatriates. The original building was built almost immediately after forming the club.

The clubs of the area competed to make the best buildings in an effort to outdo their neighboring clubs. The Italian Club, the German Club and others all tried to make the most impressive structures they could with the limited resources they had. All were designed to show off the cultural heritage of their members. All the clubs were built by the very artisans they were formed to help in their mutual aid societies. It also gave the clubs very unique architectures.

A great fire in 1916 destroyed the Cuban Club and damaged several other nearby buildings. The Cuban Club used the fire to spur on new construction of a grand new building for the organization. The building just celebrated its 100th birthday in 2017 and still stands as a towering feature of the historic Ybor City neighborhood in Tampa.

Burgert Brothers photo of the Cuban Club in 1926. *Tampa–Hillsborough County Public Library System.*

The yellow brick building is three stories high, with a small double-sided staircase, and sits on the corner of Palm Avenue and Fourteenth Street in Tampa. Between two tall columns, just above the door, is a sign that reads, "El Circulo Cubano," which translates as "Circle of Cubans." The stained-glass window above the door prominently displays the Cuban flag.

Imported tile and stained-glass windows decorate the entire structure. It currently contains a two-story theater, a pharmacy, a library, a ballroom and a cantina. The grand ballroom ceiling once displayed artistic murals and was known for its elaborately carved decorations along the walls. There was also once a swimming pool and gym in the area now housing the cantina. At one point, the building even had two bowling lanes.

Twenty-five cents got a whole family access to the club for a month. Plays, dances, boxing matches and cigars were covered by the membership fee. Even the entire family's prescriptions were covered by the dues. It is often cited as one of the first HMOs in the country.

Next to the impressive Cuban Club building is the Courtyard. This area has hosted many famous entertainers, including Glenn Miller and Tommy Dorsey, and even continues to host events to this day. At one point, a boxing ring was erected to host prizefights. Cuban entertainers such as Benny More and Celia Cruz frequently played at the site.

The club was owned by various board members until the mid-1990s. Membership peaked at near three thousand members back in the 1930s. However, over the next half century, it declined until its membership reached merely a few hundred. It was finally turned into a nonprofit organization. It has recently begun efforts to further restore the building.

Today, the site primarily hosts events. Many bands perform there quite frequently, usually on the cantina's stage or in the theater above. It hosts lavish parties and weddings for those who want a taste of Cuban Club elegance. The cantina in the building is a very popular bar in Ybor City and is frequently at capacity with weekend crowds.

Every ghost tour in Tampa stops by this building. The Travel Channel named it one of the top ten most haunted buildings in America. What makes

The ballroom of the Cuban Club in 1926. *Tampa–Hillsborough County Public Library System.*

this building so haunted? Workers at the Cuban Club speak of elevators running by themselves. Some smell the smoky odor of the original building's fire. Some hear or see the ghost of a little boy who drowned in the pool long ago while working in the cantina, where the pool once was located. Disembodied voices, echoing laughter and even haunting music can all be heard floating through the grand ballroom when it is supposed to be empty.

Almost everyone agrees that the most haunted room at the Cuban Club is the theater. According to legend, an actor and playwright in 1929 could not remember the words to his own play. Instead of dying of embarrassment, he decided to take his own life. Some versions of the story say that he shot and killed himself on stage. Other versions state that he came back later and hanged himself from the lighting. Either way, he met a most gruesome end.

His ghost is frequently spotted on or close to the stage. One witness stated that he had seen the ghostly man in the mirror of a nearby men's restroom, and he explained his whole story in English and then repeated it in Spanish. The man said that the actor stepped through the wall from behind the mirror and into the room with him. He panicked and fled. As he told us this tale, the

The Cuban Club as it stands today. *Author's photo.*

hair on his arms were standing on end. He reported that he has never gone back to the Cuban Club and never will.

A recent effort to restore the building to much of its original glory has been stymied—not by spirits but by the United States government. Though in the National Register of Historic Places, the site has had trouble with its assets being frequently frozen. Having the word *Cuban* in its name triggers flags for transactions by many financial institutions until it can be researched by bank officials or the U.S. Treasury Department's Office of Foreign Assets Control.

Structural repairs costing more than $2 million are currently planned for the building. Sadly, the red flags delay or suspend many transactions, which in turn hinders the reconstruction efforts. The building is truly remarkable, and the ghosts would probably enjoy seeing the place back to its full glory.

There are still more ghost stories to be told about the Cuban Club. If you would like to know them, we highly recommend *Haunted Ybor City* by Deborah Fretham, also from The History Press.

THE SHAMAN OF PHILIPPE PARK, SAFETY HARBOR

*T*he common version of the story of Philippe Park begins in 1832, when a native of Lyon, France, acquired a large parcel of Florida land in what is now known as Safety Harbor. Count Odet Philippe made arrangements to move most of his businesses to Florida and had a plantation prepared before setting sail himself several years later. He was a childhood friend of Napoleon and a nephew of King Louis XVI. He had become a skilled surgeon. He would use his talents to help train the early European settlers of Tampa Bay in the medical arts. He had been the guiding hand who helped build the early society of what was called *Passe aux Grilleurs*, now called Pass-a-Grille.

Except most of that isn't true. What is true is that Odet Philippe was born in Lyon. His nobility titles as well as his elite birth have no historical records and are therefore highly unlikely. Being born in 1787 also means that he probably had zero connections to Napoleon, who was born in 1769. His training as a doctor is also in doubt.

We do know that Philippe made his first homestead in the United States in Charleston, South Carolina. He filed to become an American citizen on December 3, 1822. He started several businesses in Charleston, including, most likely, some questionable business dealings in the slave trade. He was noted as a "quack doctor" by locals, which could be where the doctor stories derive from. What makes these more remarkable is that Odet Philippe was most likely a black man.

His businesses in Charleston apparently dried up, and he headed for South Florida. There are records of him in the town of New River, which is now Fort Lauderdale. He left sometime shortly before the Cooley

The mound at Phillipe Park. *Author's photo.*

Massacre of 1836, which started the Second Seminole War, and fled to Key West.

Having little money when he first arrived in Key West, it is amazing that things suddenly turned around for Odet. There are stories of him once again falling into slave trading and helping to smuggle the illegal human cargo with the infamous pirate John Gomez. Though not substantiated, it would be a likely source of quick income in the then mostly destitute Florida Keys.

The Second Seminole War raged, and Philippe and many others went to Tampa Bay for protection and business opportunities. The United States government was looking for settlers to monitor the coastline, and Odet became the custodian of 165 acres along Tampa Bay. He stayed there the rest of his days. He called the land St. Helena. He named it after the island in the South Atlantic where his idol Napoleon had been placed in exile. This is most likely where the Napoleon connection comes from. This also marked the first European settlement on the Pinellas peninsula.

He had made some money in Charleston and Key West in the cigar industry, so he brought the trade with him to Tampa. He is credited with building the foundation that would make Tampa known as the Cigar City. On his plantation, he also introduced a new citrus to the area: grapefruit. He is noted in the Florida Citrus Hall of Fame for this. Odet Philippe's grapefruit would spread throughout the bay area, and to this day, grapefruit accounts for one-fifth of all the citrus production of Florida.

The grave of Odet Philippe. *Author's photo.*

During a terrible hurricane in 1848, Odet fled to a mound that sat on the edge of his property. This large mound helped shield his plantation and helped him survive the storm. Although extensive rebuilding of his plantation was needed, he noted that the storm seemed to give the mound a wide berth.

Why did the storm spare his plantation when so many others nearby were destroyed? The mound had been there for as long as Odet had inhabited the area. He had thought little of it except as a place of shelter and primarily used it as a lookout point for ships in the bay, but it had saved his life and his livelihood. He never learned the legend of the mound, but we do know that he is buried somewhere near the mound. A marker for him still rests less than one hundred feet from the mound in the modern-day park that bears his name, Philippe Park in Safety Harbor.

The Temple Mound had been most likely built by the Native American tribe called the Tocobaga Indians. The mound is made of alternating layers of shell and sand. The remains of posts have been found on the top of the mound, indicating that at some point there was at least one building on the top of the mound. Archaeologists believe it was either for ceremonial purposes or a chief or high priest's dwelling. There are also remains of a ramp that led to what was once a village.

Although no one has been able to determine how big the village at the site once was, it is estimated to have housed thousands of people for several hundred years between AD 900 and the late 1600s. Spanish explorers recorded the area as the "capital city" of the Tocobaga tribe.

Historians know quite a bit about the Tocobaga Indians. They primarily were famous for using tattoos to identify their societal rank. Some historical documents remarked on Tocobaga Indians having their tattoos removed if they were marked incorrectly. This would be long before laser surgery.

When the Spanish came to the peninsula in the 1500s, they interacted with the tribe of this area frequently. One conquistador, Pánfilo de Narváez, landed in Pinellas in 1528. He pillaged most of the Tocobagan lands and destroyed most of their villages and huts. There are stories of the Spaniard cutting off the nose of the local chief and feeding the chief's mother to his pet war dogs.

The Tocobagans disappeared shortly after 1565, where their last account at the site details a peace accord between them and the Calusa tribe to their south. This peace accord was brokered by Pedro Menéndez de Avilés, the founder of St. Augustine on the other coast of Florida. It would be the last time the mound was mentioned by anyone until Odet Philippe arrived more than two hundred years later. The tribe was likely devastated by European diseases and war. Most of the survivors most likely merged with the other tribes of Florida.

The stories of the mound protecting the lands around it still ring out. There are stories of a mighty shaman of the Tocobaga who could command a great spirit of the land. The shaman would climb to the top of the mound

The shaman summons the spirit of the earth to protect the land from water and storm spirits that would seek to harm the resting places of the dead of Tampa Bay. *Illustration by Kari Schultz.*

at sunset and bless the bay. He would then call forth the giant spirit of the land to protect the settlement from the storm gods that so wanted to flood the lands. The frequent afternoon thunderstorms of the area are said to be the battles of these great spirits.

Paranormal enthusiasts and historians are drawn to this park. Ghostly shadows, perhaps from the old village long gone, are said to dash among the moss-laden trees of Philippe Park. Odet Philippe's ghost is said to wander the lands of his old plantation. Some even say that the old shaman is seen marching up the mound every night at sunset to continue his blessing and protection of the bay. Could his blessing be the reason Tampa Bay dodges so many deadly storms?

The park opened in 1948 and became the first historical landmark in Florida. It is a common place for weddings and picnics. In 1979, stone walls were built around the mound to help prevent erosion and deter the removal of any relics of the Tocobaga tribe. If you find any artifacts at the park, please report to park officials. Besides, you don't want to upset the shaman. The storm gods might win if he doesn't summon the earth spirit guardian of Tampa Bay.

THE OLDEST RESIDENT OF TAMPA BAY, ST. PETERSBURG

St. Petersburg was founded by two gentlemen who had purchased the land in 1876. John Contantine Williams Sr. was a Detroit man with crippling asthma. He was told by his doctors that he should move to Florida for his health. He purchased a few parcels of land all over Tampa Bay, including most of the Pinellas peninsula. He moved to Tampa and began to improve the lands across the bay to prepare it for settlement.

Pytor Alexeyevitch Dementyev was a Russian aristocrat and former captain of the Imperial Guard. Fleeing Russia after the assassination of Czar Alexander II in 1881, he moved to America and took the name Peter Demens. Not pleased with New York, he headed for a cousin's orange grove in Florida. He originally invested in lumber. When the Orange Belt Railway could not pay him for railroad ties in 1885, Demens took over its charter. He became a railroad baron overnight.

Williams pleaded with Demens to bring the Orange Belt Railway to his new settlement in Tampa Bay in exchange for plots of land there. Demens teamed up with Hamilton Disston, and the two brought the railway, which eventually connected Jacksonville, Kissimmee and Tampa Bay.

On June 8, 1888, the final railway stretch of line was completed and opened to Williams's settlement. There was no name for this peninsula, so when the train finally arrived, Demens and Williams decided to name the town after their childhood homes. Legend has it that Demens won a coin toss, and so St. Petersburg, Florida, was named after Saint Petersburg, Russia. The city was almost called New Detroit.

St. Petersburg was the end of the line for the railroad. As such, the city became designed as a destination. It had no industrial base as did the more commercial city of Tampa, just across the bay. Those early developers saw it as a relaxing place to visit in the winter months. Hotels began to spring up, including one that Demens built for Williams that was called the Detroit Hotel.

Eventually, industry did arrive in the growing town. Hibbs Fish Company was established at the end of the railroad pier that extended out into the shipping channel. By 1900, the company was shipping more than one ton of fish every day. The shipping channel near the pier was dredged deeper to allow for larger shipping. Better port facilities were also built to support the growing businesses of the area.

St. Petersburg made history in 1914, when Tony Jannus and his Benoist XIV flying boat instituted regular service across Tampa Bay. This made it the first scheduled commercial airline flight. It delivered mail and the occasional passenger across Tampa Bay.

The city prospered during the 1920s, as did most of Florida. While the rest of the United States was suffering from the Great Depression, Florida became a place for cheap living and warm winters. The population of the state began to grow exponentially.

In the 1920s, the circus business came to St. Petersburg. John Ringling and his world-renowned circus had already made a name for its winter headquarters in Sarasota, just south of St. Petersburg. Other smaller circuses flocked to the area hoping to get cast-off acts or to attempt to steal attractions from the larger circus. This led to the area around Tampa Bay to become a circus boomtown. This also led to the town of Gibsonton across the bay becoming famous as a haven for sideshow acts.

In 1922, the contents of one such traveling circus and carnival was on a boat at the St. Petersburg Pier and could not pay its dock fees. The story goes that the captain of the boat decided to sell one of the carnival's exhibits to the pier, which was operated by the local government. He hoped that this would cover his expenses and they could be on their way. The port authority agreed and took the exhibit in exchange for the port fees. The curios artifact was filed away for the time being.

In the 1930s, private company pensions and the new Social Security program provided a new way of life for the elderly population of the United States. Instead of moving back in with children, or multi-generational homes, senior citizens could now move to warmer climes. Many came to St. Petersburg, where their money would go further and the winds between the Gulf and Tampa Bay kept the humidity a bit under control.

St. Petersburg suddenly became a retirement community. It gained fame across the nation as the place where your grandparents could live in a small home on the bus line. The town quickly became known for its shuffleboard club and the booming Webb's City Drugstore, which was basically a precursor to the big-box stores of today.

The city began to install its famous green benches along the city streets. These were mostly used as places for the elderly to sit and relax in the sun. The weather was always warm, and the living was cheap. This status quo proved to be both a blessing and a curse for the city.

For a long time, St. Petersburg became "the old folks city." The rest of the world had moved on, but St. Petersburg became lost in time. The booms and busts that changed the state over the next century seemed to have little effect on the Sunshine City. It had developed an image of being too old-fashioned. The image of old people living on fixed incomes wasn't easy to shake.

Sometime in the early 2000s, things began to change. More and more young people started moving into the city, as the housing there was cheaper than in most other places in Florida. A large artistic community full of cultural diversity began to take hold. An entrepreneurial spirit filled the town. New restaurants and shopping experiences seemed to open daily. The city has been busy reinventing itself.

As for the curious circus artifact, well, it has an interesting history as well. The carnival had been showcasing it all along the Mississippi River during the early '20s. The discovery of King Tutankhamun's tomb in 1922 led to a worldwide fascination with Ancient Egypt, dubbed "Egyptmania." Every museum, sideshow and circus did everything they could to get their hands on a mummy. This one was no exception.

After being taken by the port authority, the mummy and its carved wooden sarcophagus changed hands several times. There are reports of the mummy being displayed in various locations throughout the city over the years. Eventually, it was donated to the St. Petersburg Museum of History.

At this time, the mummy had been placed in a small Victorian toe-pincher coffin. The sarcophagus was clearly not actually the mummy's, as it appeared to be of a different age then the mummy itself. It would not be until the 1970s that attempts were made to identify what the museum had already called "Our Lady of the Nile."

The mummy was X-rayed and CAT-scanned. The skeleton showed that she was a woman who had died between the ages of thirty and thirty-five. The materials and methods used to mummify her helped conclude that she had been buried nearly three thousand years ago. This would mark her as one of the oldest mummies. She had been mummified in one of the earliest types of the mummification ritual.

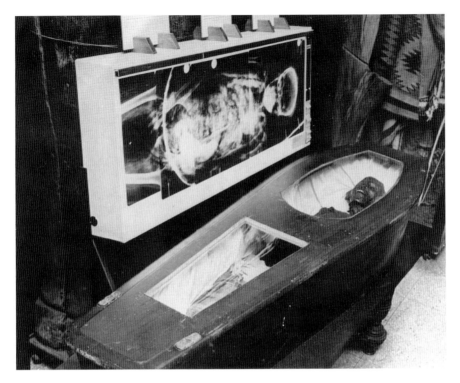

"Our Lady of the Nile" at the St. Petersburg Museum of History gets an X-ray. *St. Petersburg Museum of History.*

After her death, the body would have been carefully slit open along the left side of her torso. All of her internal organs would have been removed. The organs would then dry and be coated with plant resin and oils. These would then be wrapped in linen cloth and placed in ceremonial "canopic jars." These would have been placed near the body inside the tomb, with the exception of the heart.

The inside of the body cavity would then be rinsed with wine or oils. A long metal rod would be inserted through the nose. This would be used to scramble the brain and allow it to drain through the nostrils. The entire body would then be packed and covered with salt for seventy days.

When the corpse had completely dehydrated, it would be removed from the salt and its internal cavity would then be packed with rolls of cloth to restore a more human appearance. The heart would be wrapped in linen and returned to the body at this time. A metal scarab emblem was placed over her heart. The scarab was the ancient Egyptian symbol of resurrection.

Her entire form then would have been wrapped in linen cloth soaked in even more oils. The mummified body would have been placed within a carved stone or wooden sarcophagus bearing her likeness. She would have been placed in a tomb with offerings to the gods and items she would need in the next life. Food, utensils, furniture and clothing were usually placed in the tomb with the mummified person.

These artifacts might have given some sense of who she was in life and her status. Having been taken out of the context of her tomb, there was no possible way to identify her. Historians do believe her to have been a very wealthy priestess, as the period of her mummification and the costs associated would have been unavailable to many others at the time.

The sarcophagus she had traveled with had also been most likely taken from a different Egyptian tomb, as it appears to be at least a hundred years, if not hundreds of years, younger than her. As the carved sarcophagus was also taken out of the context of its own tomb, identification of the true owner of it will be nearly impossible to determine. The mummy and sarcophagus are now on permanent display at the St. Petersburg Museum of History. It lies just beside the fateful pier where the pair were sold to pay for passage.

The museum houses several other exhibits that rotate frequently. Notable exhibits from St. Petersburg history include one of the famous green benches. Another is a strange stuffed two-headed calf that had been born in nearby Safety Harbor in 1925. The museum even houses a full-sized replica of the Benoist XIV airplane. As the oldest museum in Pinellas County, having opened in 1921, it has extensive archives that have drawn researchers from all over the world.

So, if you visit the growing arts districts or just the vast sunny beaches of St. Petersburg, be sure to visit its many museums. The St. Petersburg Museum of Fine Arts has constantly rotating exhibits. The unique Salvador Dali Museum showcases the works of the namesake artist. The Morean Arts Center houses the world-famous Chihuly Collection. All of these make for amazing experiences when you want to get out of the sun for a few hours.

However, don't forget to make a stop at the St. Petersburg Museum of History. Look at some of its unique exhibits. Currently, it houses the largest autographed baseball collection in the world. You might be able to see the two-headed calf. You might even be able to see the infamous brassiere that figured prominently in a money embezzlement scam from the early phone company that was so infamous it was featured on *Mysteries at the Museum* on the History Channel. Just make sure to say hi to St. Petersburg's oldest resident, "Our Lady of the Nile."

SOLOMON'S CASTLE, ONA

*T*here's a great bit in *Monty Python and the Holy Grail* from 1975 when a king is talking to his son about their home, Swamp Castle: "Everyone said it was daft to build a castle in the swamp, but I built it all the same—just to show 'em."

When visiting Central Florida and the very off-the-beaten-path town of Ona, you'll find a castle standing tall in the middle of a Florida swamp. It shines brilliantly in the sun, complete with a moat and docked pirate ship next to it. The construction of this marvel began before that movie even came out.

A sculptor, woodcarver, metalworker and author began working on this castle in 1972. This is even more amazing since they were all just one man: the artist Howard Solomon. Howard moved back to the States from the Bahamas looking for a quiet place to retire and work on his crafts. When he discovered that the cheap land he had purchased was mostly swamp, he decided to make the most of it.

The castle began in earnest in 1974, when the local newspaper ran an advertisement that it was selling sheets of its aluminum printing plates for ten cents per. The ad noted that they could be used for fixing up chicken coops or sheds. Howard went and bought several hundred sheets. He would continue to buy them for years. The paper eventually just began to give them to him. Years later, the three-story, twelve-thousand-square-foot structure is the castle that gleams like a beacon in the brilliant Florida sun. It is simply breathtaking.

Solomon's Castle shines in the Florida sun. *Author's photo.*

The castle serves a dual purpose as a house for Solomon and his family as well as a museum filled with some of his art. He loved to boast that these were the pieces that "didn't sell." Many of the works are copies of the works of other artists but done entirely in scrap wood. Other pieces are complete creations made from recycled metal parts.

Most of the art pieces involve puns, as Howard titled most of his works with incredibly pun-filled names. For instance, outside the castle are two suits of armor guarding the door. One is a white knight and the other a black knight. Howard called them "Knight and Day." Inside there is a board with dinosaur sculptures crossing it. He said they were too poor to own Jurassic Park, so they made "Jurassic Plank." A large Egyptian barge made out of recycled materials sits on one wall. Only half is there, as "Cleopatra lost the other half in the divorce." These puns and oftentimes groan-inducing jokes are gleefully pointed out by the colorful tour guides at the castle.

Later parts of the tour lead you into some of the Solomon family's living quarters, with stained-glass windows carved by the master artist himself. Several hundred pieces of art and pun-filled displays dazzle you throughout

The Boat in the Moat. *Author's photo.*

the castle. One of the gadgets built into the castle is an electric elevator made of scrap material in the kitchen and operated by a car battery.

Outside the castle is the Boat in the Moat restaurant. This full-size replica of a sixteenth-century Spanish galleon is resplendent with more stained-glass windows and the ever-impressive woodworking craftsmanship of Howard Solomon. Masts, sails, cannons and rigging fill the decks. The heavenly aroma of well-cooked food floats throughout the boat, as the restaurant there serves delicious treats for visitors to the castle.

When Hurricane Irma came through in 2017, the water levels in the normally very low Horse Creek were finally high enough to reach the bottom floors of the boat. We are happy to report that the Boat in the Moat weathered the storm, as did the castle. This may have been due to the "Lily Light" lighthouse that Howard had built next to the boat to help with overflow from the restaurant. He built the house using primarily balsa wood because he wanted to make the lighthouse a light house.

Sadly, in 2016, at the age of eighty-one, the man known as the "Da Vinci of Debris," the "Rembrandt of Reclamation" and the "Savior of Salvage"— or Howard to his friends—passed away. He had continued working up until the very end. His castle stands as a shining example of what one man can build—quite literally shining in the sun.

Today, the castle is run by Howard's family and still hosts weddings, parties and gatherings. The twenty-minute walk-around nature trail through the swamp is quite breathtaking, and you'll stumble on even more of Howard's sculptures and collections of oddities, like his replica Alamo complete with a bowling ball–firing cannon. You can't help but smile at Solomon's Castle. Just make sure to gas up before you go. It's a long way to the castle in the swamp but well worth the drive.

BLOODY BUCKET BRIDGE, WAUCHULA

*I*n the middle of Florida, there is an area off the beaten path of tourists. Southwest of Lake Seminole and northwest of Lake Okeechobee is an area many call the "Florida plains." This area is notable for little-known towns and forgotten homesteads. It is crisscrossed with small roads that lead to old farms and quarries. Ghost towns like Popash once dotted the area. Now with Florida's growing population, even this area is expanding and developing quickly. The once abandoned heart of Florida is beating again.

Every ghost town and abandoned building in the area has some haunted history with it. For a long while, an abandoned school stood on Popash Road. Stories circulated similar to the ones surrounding Jacksonville's Devil's School. Though easily debunked, the legends persisted until the school was finally demolished.

One legend here lives on, though. On Griffin Road, there was a bar in the '30s called the Bloody Bucket. This bar closed in the '40s, when the county where it was located went "dry," preventing the sale of alcohol. The ruined bar lasted for years until it was destroyed by either a strong storm or vandals. No one is really sure how it finally collapsed. The road, though, is still unofficially called "Bloody Bucket Road," and the bridge next to the bar is called the "Bloody Bucket Bridge."

Most locals say that the bridge and road were named after the bar. Others say the bar was named after the legend of the bridge. While it doesn't take long to find someone willing to tell the legend, it takes even less time to find

The bridge most often associated with Bloody Bucket Road. *Author's photo.*

somebody in the area to point you to the bridge and the concrete slab where the bar once stood.

The legend in question involves an ex-slave moving to the area in the mid-1870s. She was a skilled midwife and helped deliver many of the children in the nearby homesteads. The population was growing, and the farmers kept having numerous children to tend their burgeoning farms. The midwife began to wonder if the area really needed so many new children.

The infant mortality rate began to climb in the area. Many of these children died in childbirth. It seems that the midwife had decided to take population control into her own hands. She would claim that the child was stillborn after suffocating the child at birth. She would then take infants away to be buried. She would explain it away as letting the family begin to grieve. The story goes that she didn't bury the children but rather dumped them in the river at an old bridge.

It didn't take long for the families to realize that a large number of these failed deliveries were attended by the same midwife. The story diverges here. Some versions say that the town rose up and threw her in the river and that the waters ran red with blood for days. Other variants of the tale say that folks simply shunned the ex-slave. She was forced into the woods to survive. There she was haunted by the spirits of the many dead children she had killed. She would often be seen dumping her delivery bucket into the water, still filled with blood. As soon as she finished pouring it into the river below,

The ghostly lady and her grim fate at the infamous Bloody Bucket Bridge. *Illustration by Kari Schultz.*

it would refill. Finally, after months of torment, she threw herself and the bucket from the bridge.

While there is no evidence to support either story, the legend is quite persistent, and numerous ghost hunters come to the area to investigate. The bridge most associated with the tale is now a two-lane bridge across the old river. It is unlikely to be at the exact spot of the old bridge, but the road there follows pre-1900 maps showing a road and bridge extremely close to that spot on the river.

In one encounter related to us by witnesses, it was said they went to the remains of the old bar to drink and have a good time. They also knew the legend of the bridge, so there was the added benefit of watching for ghostly apparitions. After a while, they got in their car and headed for home. A police officer pulled them over a short distance away from the bridge. The group was convinced they were in serious trouble.

When the officer leaned into the car and shined his light on one of the ladies in the back seat, his face went pale white. He asked them where the child was. Puzzled, the group asked, "What child?" He claimed that he had pulled them over because he had seen the lady holding a baby in the backseat. He had stopped them to have them put the child in a car seat. He was visibly shaken, as the group had no child at all in the car. He staggered back and sent them on their way.

The group of partiers were initially pleased with their good luck being set loose. Then they realized the implications of the officer's assumption. Had they been paid a visit by one of the murdered children of Bloody Bucket Bridge?

As for which came first, the legend or the bar, we'll probably never know. The story goes that if you head out to the old bridge on a full moon, the waters will run red with blood. Ghostly children are seen in the area, and the disembodied cries of infants can be heard echoing across the waters. With all the developments expanding near there, it is not out of the realm of possibility that some gruesome evidence of this legend may yet turn up.

APOLLO 1 COMPLEX, CAPE CANAVERAL

Construction began in 1959 for NASA's Launch Complex 34 (LC-34). It was going to be the starting point for many missions into space for generations of American astronauts. In 1961, it held its first successful launch of a Saturn I rocket. Three more unmanned Saturn I rockets were launched from the facility over the next few years.

The Apollo program had been designed to land humans on the moon and bring them safely back to Earth. This lofty goal, set by President John F. Kennedy, had been pushing the staff at NASA and its contractors to the limit. The previous programs, Mercury and Gemini, had begun the journey toward that goal. These flights of the early astronauts tested how humans behaved in space. They also would test the technical procedures needed to successfully complete the later Apollo missions.

In 1962, NASA began to modify the launch complex to host the Saturn IB program. By 1966, the modifications were completed. Two launches from the complex were successful over the next short period of time of the new Saturn IB rockets. The first manned mission in the Apollo program was planned for February 1967.

The crew was picked from the list of astronauts. Crew commander for Apollo 1 would be Virgil "Gus" Grissom. An air force veteran from the Korean War, Gus was chosen as one of the first seven astronauts of the Mercury program known as the Mercury 7. In 1961, Grissom became America's second person in space. An accident occurred when he touched down in the ocean and the hatch door of his Mercury capsule blew open for unknown reasons. The spacecraft sank and would not be recovered from the ocean floor until 1999.

Many felt that Gus had blown the hatch, though he swore it just exploded open. Some felt that his career as an astronaut would never recover. He went on to successfully command the first Gemini flight, Gemini 3. He was selected again to lead the first Apollo flight.

He was joined by fellow veteran astronaut Ed White. Ed was an air force lieutenant colonel and was also the first American to walk in space. His mission of Gemini 4 in 1965 is considered by many to be one of the most iconic missions in all of space history, as his twenty-three-minute walk in space is still frequently seen today in NASA recordings.

The third member of the team was to be Roger Chaffee. Though a seasoned navy lieutenant commander who had been in the space program since 1963, he was still considered a rookie, as he had never flown a mission in space. He had spent years promoting the space program and was the voice of CapCom on Gemini 4 with Ed White. He was finally getting a chance to fly.

Every astronaut in the Apollo program was a pilot, and many were test pilots. Most had seen development delays on prototype flight vehicles. Many had helped assess airplane readiness for some historic test programs. Most agreed that the Apollo command module just wasn't ready yet. Engineering changes were still underway even as tests continued.

On a visit home to Texas in early 1967, Gus grabbed a lemon from a tree in his backyard. His wife, Betty, asked him why. "I'm going to hang it on the spacecraft," he replied as he kissed her goodbye. Back in Cape Canaveral, he hung it on the flight simulator.

A practice countdown test was scheduled for the morning of January 27, 1967. The crew suited up and went to the tower to board the spacecraft. The crew detected a foul odor in their oxygen supply that took some time to correct. The countdown test was put on hold, and the men stayed in the ship. Hours passed, and communications systems began to act up. Grissom shouted through the garbled communications, "How are we going to get to the moon if we can't talk between two or three buildings?"

As these problems dragged on, the countdown was again held. Then, at 6:31 p.m., a word many never wanted to hear came over the garbled communications: "Fire." Deke Slayton, who oversaw all the crew selections at NASA, was present for the test. He saw the flames on the closed-circuit television and saw the ground crew struggling to get the astronauts out.

Grissom, White and Chaffee pose for a gag photo before testing the AS-204 launch vehicle. *NASA Archives.*

The door to the spacecraft was opened eventually, but it was too late for the crew of Apollo 1.

NASA review found that a stray spark in the pure oxygen environment of the capsule had caused the fire. Fed by flammable features like nylon netting, Velcro and foam pads, the blaze spread extremely quickly. The hatch door to the command module had been unmovable, as the pressure from the fire made it nearly impossible to open.

The reviews by NASA and later the U.S. Senate would create a list of recommendations that would alter the space program to this day. The astronauts and contractors now worked together concerning design changes. The hatch door was completely redesigned. Lives have been saved.

It would be eighteen months, and there were extensive redesigns, before NASA would launch more men into space. The complex at LC-34 also received numerous firefighting tools and was completely redesigned from the ground up.

On October 11, 1968, the first manned Apollo launch, Apollo 7, was launched from LC-34. It was to be the last time the site was used. It was

Apollo 7 launches into space at launch site C-34 just over a year after the Apollo 1 disaster. *NASA Archives.*

decommissioned in 1971. The umbilical tower and service structure were demolished shortly after decommissioning. The site sat abandoned for decades. The only structure remaining on the site was the launch platform standing at the center of the launch pad. Today, it serves as a memorial to the crew of Apollo 1 with the following dedication plaque:

LAUNCH COMPLEX 34
Friday, 27 January 1967
1831 Hours

Dedicated to the living memory of the crew of the Apollo 1

U.S.A.F. Lt. Colonel Virgil I. Grissom
U.S.A.F. Lt. Colonel Edward H. White II
U.S.N. Lt. Commander Roger B. Chaffee

They gave their lives in service to their country in the ongoing exploration of humankind's final frontier. Remember them not for how they died but for those ideals for which they lived.

You can still visit the site today by arranging a tour through the Cape Canaveral Visitor Center. Paranormal experts and urban explorers often sneak onto the site looking for a ghostly astronaut often seen there. The ghost is so famous that it was even featured on the show *Doctor Who*. While these sightings are notable, it is the solemnity and history of the site itself that make a visit worthwhile.

BLACK WATER HATTIE AND THE LAKE OF THE DEAD, LAKE OKEECHOBEE

Lake Okeechobee is Florida's largest lake and the second-largest body of fresh water in the contiguous United States (only Lake Michigan is larger). The lake went by many names among the early inhabitants of the area. The oldest known name was Mayaimi, which meant "big water" to the Calusa Indians. This was reported by a Spanish shipwreck survivor who lived among the natives of Florida for many years in the mid-1500s. It is believed that this word is probably where the city of Miami gets its name.

Spanish and English explorers referred to the great inland sea as "Sarrope" or "Lake Mayacco." The Spanish often called it *Laguna del Esperita Santo*. Lake Okeechobee got its current name from the Seminole Indian word also meaning "big water." The lake covers about seven hundred square miles. It is unusually shallow for such a large lake. The average depth is less than ten feet, and the maximum depth is less than twenty feet. The lake refills from the massive amount of rainfall typical of Florida and some from the Kissimmee River to the north.

In 1926 and again in 1928, hurricanes came through the areas along the southern shores, destroying dikes that had been built to contain the lake. These storms resulted in thousands of deaths around the lake. The U.S. Army Corps of Engineers and the South Florida Water Management District now use a series of dikes, canals and floodgates to prevent further tragedies. These protection systems also help to prevent saltwater intrusion and allow for agricultural irrigation near the lake. These waters also are a large part of the drinking water supply for much of South Florida.

Some of these waters are absorbed into the soil, which helps create much of the swamplands around the lake. Before the water management began, these waters would begin the flow of the Everglade's "River of Grass"—shallow waters ranging from only a few inches wide and a few feet in depth to some over fifty miles wide. They slowly flowed more than one hundred miles to the south into the Gulf of Mexico and Florida Bay, helping to create the unique ecosystem of the Florida Everglades.

The lake is no stranger to crazy stories and legends. Even early explorers were told by their Native American guides that the lake had many monsters, including a giant alligator god that lived deep in the heart of the lake. Shortly after Florida became a part of the United States in the 1800s and settlement began in force, the area around the lake saw a huge population boom, mostly thanks to so much available fresh water.

Early pioneers, though, found something unusual in the area: piles and piles of human bones. Local papers reported of fishermen finding skulls in their nets. While surveying was occurring in an area called Grassy Island in the early 1900s, the clearing of said land revealed a large collection of skeletons with merely an inch or two of sand covering them. Apparently, it was a common sight to see piles of skulls and bones when the water levels were down.

A record low water level in Lake Okeechobee occurred in 1918. Large quantities of piled human remains were discovered in the swampy silt of the lake numbering in the hundreds. Mostly these remains were along the islands that dot the lake, but many more along the lake bottom were now revealed. Some researchers feel these were the victims of some ancient hurricane.

Historians and archaeologists are uncertain as to why there are so many remains, as little to no artifacts have been found with the bodies. Some believe that the site was merely a spiritual burial site, but the lack of artifacts seems odd. The bodies were scattered all over the lake, with no apparent rhyme or reason. Many were removed or reburied with little thought for archaeological preservation, so we may likely never know why the lake was filled with so many dead.

One famous legend told throughout the cities that border the lake is that of a swamp witch named Black Water Hattie. The tale tells of an early pioneer town along the lake that had a bad outbreak of the most dreaded of all diseases in Florida: yellow fever.

The town had known about Hattie and her shack for generations. She lived not far from town, but deep enough into the swamp to discourage visitors. Some of the locals went to seek out Hattie for charms and even

Black Water Hattie lived back in the woods, where the strange green reptiles roamed.
Illustration by Kari Schultz.

healing potions over the years. Many in town now felt that they had been dealing with the devil and that Hattie had brought their plague to the town. A lynch mob began to form.

As dawn broke, though, a strange cauldron of a foul-smelling liquid was found in the center of town. A few brave souls drank at the strange mixture and were suddenly cured. The whole town drank heartily, and everyone in town was miraculously cured. The lynch mob quickly turned into a search party to go find and thank Hattie. Somehow, though, they couldn't find her. The trails twisted and seemed to have changed while they searched the swamp. The only thing the searchers found was a simple note that read, "Don't come lookin' again."

While traveling for this book, we heard this same story told in several towns in the area. Many claimed to be the descendants of the townsfolk in question. Others claimed that Hattie still lives in the black swamp near their town and is more than two hundred years old. In truth, this really can't be the case.

Hattie came from the fertile imagination of a singer/songwriter in 1974. Jim Stafford was born and raised in Winter Haven, Florida, not far from Lake Okeechobee. He played in a band with several friends and had some local success. Sometime in the early 1970s, he sat down to write a song about a swamp witch who tried to help a town that didn't want help. The song, "Swamp Witch," cracked the U.S. Top 40 in July 1973. Black Water Hattie became a household legend.

Jim Stafford sings his hit song "Swamp Witch" about Black Water Hattie. *Jim Stafford.*

We got to talk to Jim Stafford while putting this book together. He was very gracious and even dug out the original "to-do" note that had simply told himself to write a song about a swamp witch with a bare-bones outline. The name Hattie came from an old lady who did live in a small shack behind the Methodist church in his hometown. "So, in a way there really was Hattie's Shack," according to the songwriter.

Going on the very next year to peak at no. 3 with the gold record "Spiders and Snakes," Jim Stafford had cemented himself as a successful singer/songwriter. He contributed music to *The Fox and the Hound* for Walt Disney Studios. He also wrote the famed song "Cow Patti" for the Clint Eastwood movie *Any Which Way You Can* and got to appear in the movie.

Jim Stafford also appeared on several TV variety shows in the mid-'70s, including *The Smothers Brothers Comedy Hour*. He was even credited as a supervising writer for that show. In 1975, *The Jim Stafford Show* premiered and ran for a while on ABC with Jim as the host. Many may also remember him as a co-host on *Those Amazing Animals* in the early '80s with Burgess Meredith and Priscilla Presley.

In 1990, Jim Stafford opened his own theater in Branson, Missouri, where he still performs. You can still hear his song "Swamp Witch" on many stations around the state. When someone tells you the tale of Black Water Hattie, you be sure to tell them that Jim Stafford thanks them for keeping the legend alive, but they really should just go buy the album or see him live in Branson or his occasional tour dates.

THE LOST PYRAMIDS OF CORKSCREW MARSH, IMMOKALEE

As long as there have been explorations of Florida's swampy interior, there have been tales of a lost civilization there. Perhaps these people were an offshoot of lost Mayans. Some say they've even stumbled on their pyramids deep in the everglades. There was one story of a pyramid built into bedrock in the middle of a swamp that contains a room filled with snakes—straight out of an *Indiana Jones* film.

Explorers have long chased stories of lost treasures of pirates along the many islands that dot the coast of Florida. Some treasure hunters turned their quests inland and tried their luck in the seemingly vast expanse of the Everglades. While the swamps of Florida do house lost relics, a lost civilization seems unlikely.

In 2014, three amateur explorers found the remnants of Fort Harrell, an 1837 outpost of the U.S. Army used during the Seminole Wars and missing for more than a century. They found it deep in the Big Cypress National Preserve. They had spent hundreds of hours researching and many more hours on foot on the ground before they discovered it.

Several famed archaeologists, including Joseph Manson Valentine, spent many years searching for the lost pyramids. Valentine, most famous for finding the unusual rock formations known as the Bimini Road, was the honorary curator of the Miami Museum of Science. But he had a shadow over much of his research for being associated with the search for the lost civilization of Atlantis.

Valentine had never made any mention of Atlantis in any of his finds, but the association by many with the Bimini Road and Atlantis was very common. This meant that Valentine himself was often associated with those who did fringe archaeological research. He did claim to have seen an unusual pyramid that he longed to research deep in a Florida swamp, but he never wrote about it in his later years.

Florida was home to many ancient civilizations, and we are only now learning how extensive their societies were. The Calusas, Tequestas, Timucuas and many others lived here long before the early Spanish explorers would land in La Florida. None of the groups were stone builders like the Central and South American cultures, though. Pyramids of stone seem very unlikely.

While working on *Eerie Florida*, we were approached by a man who claimed to know where a lost pyramid could be found. It was in the heart of the Corkscrew Marsh. The man gave us extensive directions, and we made arrangements to travel to the swamp.

The Corkscrew Regional Ecosystem Watershed (CREW) is a swamp sanctuary along the northwestern boundary of Corkscrew Marsh. The CREW Marsh Trail Loop leads to an observation tower that overlooks the pine flatwoods, oak hammocks and palm forests of the area. It is a very remote area, and the trail system is nearly always flooded during the wet seasons.

The map we were given showed the area of three mounds in a row that might match a map of the pyramids at Giza in Egypt. Feeling that the pyramid of a lost civilization being just off a nature trail seemed unlikely,

A view of a small midden in a lake at Corkscrew Marsh—a far cry from the promised pyramid. *Author's photo.*

The Pyramids of Florida in Fort Meyers represent a unique hotel experience. *Author's photo.*

we went anyway. Sorry to say that we did not find any lost civilizations. No pyramids were found on our march through the beautiful CREW Marsh Trail Loop. Even at the impressive overlook, we saw a beautiful landscape but no signs of Atlantis.

The legends of this lost civilization may boil down to simple racism. Early explorers felt that the Native America tribes of Florida were nowhere near as advanced as those to the south, as they hadn't built anything the size and scope of the Mayans, the Toltecs or the Aztecs—mostly this was due to a lack of useable rock in Florida. Instead, the tribes here built with shell and mud. The mounds here were huge and impressive complexes that are all still scattered throughout the state.

Elsewhere in this book, you'll read about the complex sites and legends around them throughout the state. The lost civilizations that made these are known. There is no need for some mythical lost city to have built these impressive archaeological structures.

However, if you would like someplace unique to stay in Florida, there are some pyramids we'd love to tell you about: the very aptly named Pyramids in Florida. Established in 1997, this collection of three-sided rental properties in Fort Meyers surrounds a natural thermal lake with soothing, mineral-rich waters. The rental pyramid chalets come in varying sizes and layouts. Each has a fully equipped kitchen and a very cozy vibe. One of the chalets is even on Airbnb with a five-star rating.

If you can't find the lost pyramids of Florida, then perhaps you can just lounge by a thermal lake and enjoy the sunshine. When you are done, you can go to bed in your own pyramid and focus that healing energy into your own homeopathic resort stay.

THE BATHTUB MESSIAH AND HOLLOW EARTH, ESTERO

*I*n southwest Florida, on I-75 between Fort Meyers and Naples, lies the quiet town of Estero. In the late nineteenth century, this land was to become a New Jerusalem. A prophet led a group of followers to this deep swampland to build a new Garden of Eden and spiritual center of learning and hope. This self-proclaimed utopia would be a new capital of a unified world. Their prophet had foreseen all of this.

Cyrus Teed was born in 1839 in New York. Growing up, he excelled in medicine and science. He opened a clinic in Utica when he became a practicing physician and at once decided to try more radical cures to help his patients. He began experiments in electricity to assist their natural healing process. In one of these experiments, he electrocuted himself.

Cyrus felt himself surrounded by a white light and was visited by a divine being. This entity told him that he was to become the new messiah. He would take the old Persian version of his name Cyrus, which was Koresh, as this meant "shepherd" in the old language. He would then find followers and lead them to a true utopia on Earth. He was also given the knowledge that we live not on a globe but inside shell of a great bubble, and the universe is contained within the confines of the Earth. The divine being gave him more knowledge on how to invent items that would prove this to the unbelievers.

Koresh Teed, as he now called himself, began to teach lectures on "Cellular Cosmogony," a variant of the Hollow Earth theory. He began to attract followers and preached about how they would live together in peace and harmony with gender equality and communal living with sharing of property. This group began in New York but quickly moved to Chicago. Many in the Windy City did not take kindly to a cult that took the property of the

Photomontage showing portraits of Dr. Cyrus Reed Teed, founder of the Koreshan Universology, and members of his family. Before 1885. *State Archives of Florida, Florida Memory.*

congregation and began to write article after article denouncing the Koreshan Unity and especially its leader, whom they still loved to call Cyrus Teed.

In 1894, the Koreshans were able to obtain acres of land in Florida through a donation from a follower. They then bartered and sold holdings to purchase even more land around the initial donation. Eventually, the site would comprise nearly 1,600 acres and would be the perfect home for their new Utopia.

In this new community, they practiced religion. Koreshanity was mostly a Christian-based religion, as it referred often to both the New and Old Testaments. It also referred quite frequently to the writings of Teed and his book *The Cellular Cosmogony: The Earth as a Concave Sphere*. The book describes his Hollow Earth theory and how the sun, moon and stars are all just giant balls of gas with a light and dark side that rotates within. Teed would lecture on the physics of this in their newly built communal hall called the Planetary Chamber.

The group's beliefs in blending science with religion gained a lot of traction in the late 1800s. Famous inventors such as Thomas Edison and Henry Ford were reportedly intrigued by some of the concepts. In many ways, the group was well ahead of the times. Women were treated as equals, as they believed in a biune God, being both male and female at the same time. This allowed them to be ahead socially in gender equality by allowing women the right to vote in church dealings many years ahead of the suffrage movement.

The Koreshan Church began to build in earnest and continued to gain followers within its New Jerusalem. The group built a bakery, a cafeteria and a theatrical art hall, as well as a sawmill, a machine shop and two general stores to help barter with visitors to the community. The group even built

Hollow Earth globe in Art Hall at Koreshan Unity in Estero, Florida. After 1905. *State Archives of Florida, Florida Memory.*

a power plant, which provided power to the area for many years before anywhere else in southwest Florida would ever get electricity. Members traded with the local community and thrived in the early 1900s. They began planning their city, anticipating that it would ultimately house 10 million followers and would include streets more than four hundred yards wide to allow for the traffic.

In 1906, Teed and the Koreshan Church decided that they needed a bigger hand in local politics and formed their own political party. The Progressive Liberty Party formed by the church believed in communal property and eagerly wanted to incorporate the little town of Estero into Lee County. The politicians of Fort Myers felt this might divert road funding from the county and fought hard against it. In October 1906, the Progressive Liberty Party, along with Cyrus "Koresh" Teed and other Unity members, were in Fort Myers to do some trading and selling of the materials they had manufactured. Local Democrats began a fight with the group, and Teed was gravely injured in the melee. The *Fort Myers News Press* followed the report with numerous editorials denouncing Teed and the Koreshans. The Koreshans printed retaliatory responses in their own paper, the *American Eagle*.

For two more years, Teed battled his injury but passed away in 1908. At this time, the Koreshans had well over 250 members at the Unity settlement in Estero and more than 4,000 members worldwide. He had prophesized that he would return on the third day after his death, just as Jesus had done before him. His followers placed him in a bathtub at the Planetary Court building, which was the building that housed all the inner sanctum members of the church and began their vigil over the body. After several days had passed, mold and decomposition crept in, and some members of the church began pointing out that it was life renewing from the old body. The health department did not agree with this and demanded Teed be buried.

Teed was buried in a crypt not far from the beach, apparently still in the bathtub. The Koreshan Church began to decline with the loss of its messiah. Several years later, a storm swept through the area, destroying the crypt. Teed's remains were never found. The church seized on this event in an attempt to revitalize itself.

Even after the supposed success of Teed's famous experiment using his own invention, a T-square–like device called a recalcinator, to prove the earth was concave, many doubted his findings. The Planetary Court building still houses a recalcinator and one of the Koreshan globes showing that we live within the earth and look inward on the universe above.

The settlement had a small boom in trade when the Tamiami Trail Highway was built and went right along the border of the church. A store was built to take advantage of the growing number of tourists, and the church began to thrive financially. With the ranks diminishing and a firm belief in reincarnation and celibacy, the Koreshans were fading fast.

The last surviving Koreshan died in 1981, after having deeded the property to the State of Florida to be made into a national park. It was opened to the public as the Koreshan Historic Site, with many of the original buildings still present on the site, as well as the beautiful grounds of what was going to be the New Jerusalem. Today, it is called Koreshan State Park after a renaming event in late 2016. Park officials wanted to keep the history of the area a priority but felt that other features like camping, hiking and nature trails were being ignored. Visitors can still walk among the old buildings and see many Koreshan artifacts. Only in Freaky Florida can you find a park that celebrates a cult that believed it was building a city at the center of Hollow Earth.

THE GIANT TURTLE OF 1932, PUNTA GORDA

Florida is famous for its endless beaches and countless tourist attractions. It's also known for the severe tropical cyclones that form in the Atlantic or the Gulf of Mexico that seem to plague the Florida peninsula every June through November. The United States National Hurricane Center monitors these storms and issues reports, watches and warnings about these deadly storms every year.

In 1932, a tropical disturbance was identified north of Hispaniola on August 26. Lacking modern-day tracking abilities, the storm was watched and reported on by ships and landfall areas. On August 30, it struck South Florida and crossed the state as what we now call a Category 1 hurricane with winds of eighty-five miles per hour. When it crossed the state and entered the Gulf of Mexico, it turned north and hugged the Florida coast for a short time while re-intensifying.

At the point of impact in South Florida, the wind damage was devastating to the state's avocado and citrus crop. As the storm regained its strength in the Gulf of Mexico, strong surf and heavy rains took a great toll all along Florida's Gulf Coast communities.

It had been hoped that the storm would go farther west and back out to sea. It did this and eventually made landfall right near the Mississippi-Alabama border. The hurricane itself caused damage in the hundreds of thousands of dollars. It is generally considered a footnote storm, as only one indirect death was attributed to it. It was clearly not one of the feared monster hurricanes that continue to plague Florida to this day.

According to an uncommon tale, however, there would have been four more deaths from the storm near the coastal town of Punta Gorda. These deaths would have certainly prompted the Florida-Alabama hurricane to be more than a footnote. The names of the people have been lost, but the story lives on in legend.

It seems that a family was living near what is now lands covered by the Charlotte Harbor Preserve State Park. The family had moved to the area during the Great Depression and was looking to make a living fishing. They had a small fishing boat that they sailed out of Charlotte Harbor to pursue the family's business.

As the hurricane barreled across the south of the state, the waters of the Gulf receded and were drawn to the storm. The family were drawn into the dry bed of Charlotte Harbor, along with many others living around Punta Gorda. The family and others took advantage of this storm, grabbing shells, oysters and crabs as fast as they could, knowing that the waters would return quickly. While not a common phenomenon, it had happened several times over the previous years.

The family strayed out farther than the rest of the town, looking for deeper treasures. The young daughter of the family of four saw what looked like a chest. Thinking of lost pirate treasure, the family made their way into the returning waters at ankle level. The chest was not easily moved from the muck of the now quickly sinking seabed. Time was not on their side.

The son was able to break the long-aged wood on the top of the chest, and they saw that it was filled with nothing but cannonballs. Perhaps a pirate or Civil War boat had lost them. Either way, they would be of little value to the family, and they took what they had caught and tried to make their way back to shore.

The storm was coming up on them, and the tide returned much faster than they had hoped. They had taken too long and traveled too far out into the Gulf of Mexico. They realized that they might have better luck trying to make it up the coast to Florida Harbor before the sea and storm returned in force.

A large wave crashed into the family, and they scrambled to hold on to one another. The mother grabbed the daughter and father the son as they were swept away, back over the very land to which they were trying to return. They landed somewhere near Myakka or Peace River in quickly rising floodwaters. They were not out of danger yet though.

With water levels still rising, they sought out high ground. The daughter's eagle eye spotted what they thought was a shell Indian mound not far. They struggled through the muck, winds and rain toward the small hope of shelter. They reached the mound as the waters of the flooding rivers surrounded its base. The story says that they clung to limited growth on the mound, including a small tree, as the river levels rose still further. The father began to pray as the water levels rose still higher, and they feared that even this mound would not be high enough to save them.

Suddenly, the ground lurched, as if the great mound had been wrenched free of the ground beneath it. They had been cast afloat. The mound raised and seemed to be floating back out toward the sea along the flooding river currents. Once again, they realized that they were in danger of being swept off into the ocean on this strange mound. Perhaps it was merely an old boat that had been covered with growth. They watched in horror,

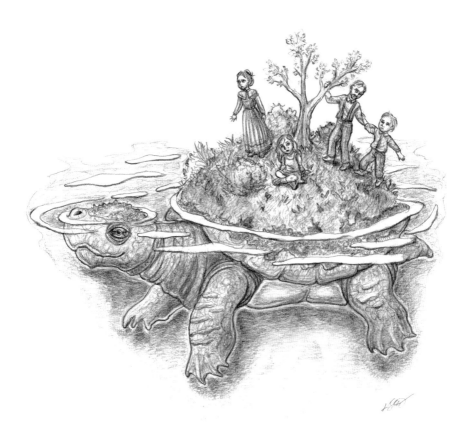

The Giant Turtle of Punta Gorda rescues a family during a hurricane. *Illustration by Kari Schultz.*

Captain Villa telling of his catch of a rare 1,400-pound leatherback turtle. 1947. *State Archives of Florida, Florida Memory.*

unable to do anything but hold on for dear life as they saw the approaching waves of the sea.

Again, the ground shifted. The mound suddenly turned away from the current. The hill was making a turn to the east and back inland. How was it fighting the current? The young boy leaned over the edge and yelled that he saw a giant flipper in the water. The daughter leaned forward and saw an extremely large turtle head. The mound was a giant turtle.

Giant animals are a common legend among the early tribes and settlers of Florida. Nearly every town has a legend of some tribal chief defeating a great serpent or alligator. There are stories of giant beasts that roam the deep waters of the Gulf and Atlantic and sometimes come ashore.

The turtle with the family riding on its back made it safely back to Punta Gorda. After their wild ride, the family apparently decided that it was time to return inland. A young man from Oklahoma told us that his grandmother had been the young girl involved with the legend. He claimed that she may have exaggerated the size of the turtle, but she swore it saved all four members of her family from that terrible storm.

Today, you can visit Charlotte Harbor Preserve State Park, which surrounds Charlotte Harbor estuary and all the major tributaries. The land there protects numerous aquatic preserves and their natural resources, including habitats for a wide variety of wildlife, including several species of turtles.

The Charlotte Harbor Environmental Center (CHEC) is located at the Alligator Creek Preserve. CHEC is known for the four miles of nature trails and the Caniff Visitors' Center. The center has a great exhibit center with information about the ecosystems within the Charlotte Harbor Preserve. It also has a fantastic gift shop filled with unique items from the area. Pick up one of the hand-carved walking sticks before heading out along the trail if you go searching for a giant turtle.

THE DEVIL'S TREE, PORT SAINT LUCIE

*I*n Port Saint Lucie, there is a nature park that is extremely difficult to find. Behind a mess of manicured lawns, beautifully developed homes and several twists and turns, you will come across the C-24 Canal boat ramp. It is now also the home to a wonderful nature trail called Oak Hammock Park. There are two trail loops here that wind their way through some beautiful old Florida woods.

Before the sea of development swarmed this area and long before Oak Hammock Park was even a park, Port Saint Lucie was very rural. It held many dirt roads that seemingly led to nowhere. It was here that a serial killer had an old house he used as his personal torture area, far away from the rest of civilization.

In 1971, a deputy for the Wilton Manors Police Department in Broward County named Gerard John Schaefer kidnapped two girls and took them to the C-24 Canal. Collette Goodenough and Barbara Ann Wilcox were out hitchhiking. Officer Schaefer flashed his badge and took them for a ride. It was the last time anyone would see them alive.

Schaefer tied the young girls to an old oak tree and raped them. He decapitated them and then began to practice several acts of necrophilia with the corpses. After he buried them at the base of the tree, he would still come out to visit the girls occasionally to continue his unspeakable acts.

Sadly, it would be years before Schaefer would face judgement for his crimes. In 1972, Schaefer, after being fired from the Wilton Manors

The Devil's Tree in Port St. Lucie. *Author's photo.*

Police Department, worked as a deputy sheriff for Broward County. It was shortly after his hiring that he had to call the sheriff and tell him that he had "done something stupid."

Schaefer claimed that he had met two hitchhiking girls and explained to them how dangerous it was to be trying to hitchhike. He then arranged to meet them the next day to take them to the beach. Instead, he told the sheriff that he had intended to put a scare into them by taking them into the woods and tying them to a tree. There he had threatened to rape them and sell them into prostitution and slavery. He had received a call and had to leave them. When he had returned, they had escaped.

The sheriff did not believe his deputy's story and had him come in. Once there, he was stripped of his badge and charged with assault and wrongful imprisonment. After making bail, he apparently struck again by kidnapping and murdering yet another pair of hitchhikers just a few months later while awaiting trial for his assault case.

In 1973, two more victims' bodies were found. The decomposing remains of Susan Place and Georgia Jessup were discovered by a man searching some woods for tin cans to recycle. The bodies had been hacked to pieces and sexually assaulted after death. The similarity to Gerard John Schaefer's current charge was more than enough to get a search warrant for his home. There they found his trophy collection.

A jewelry box was found filled with trinkets from dozens of victims. They found diaries and journals filled with stories of torture and rape. This combined with more evidence was all the proof a jury needed to convict Gerard John Schaefer for the murders of Jessup and Place. The police announced from all the evidence collected that he was connected to at least thirty other missing person cases.

The sad thing is that Place and Jessup may not have even been his final victims. Two fourteen-year-old girls had gone missing in October 1973 while hitchhiking. Their bodies were discovered later, and police believed that some of their jewelry was among the pieces found in Schaefer's home. Closer examination led to the identification of teeth of an old childhood friend of Schaefer's named Hainline Bonadies, who had disappeared in 1969.

While publicly stating that he had been framed, Schaefer went on to work with a true crime author named Sondra London, whom he had dated back in high school. Together they published a collection of short stories and his drawings called *Killer Fiction*. A few years later, a follow-up book called *Beyond Killer Fiction* came out, including more stories and copies of his letters to London. In these letters, he talked about his rivalry with fellow inmate and infamous serial killer Ted Bundy.

In his letters, Schaefer fictionally confessed to more than eighty deaths. He filed numerous lawsuits while serving his two life sentences. Some say he did this out of boredom. Others felt that he was too dangerous and might find some legal loophole to get free and kill again.

Schaefer was killed by a fellow inmate in 1995. Vincent Rivera stabbed him numerous times and took out Schaefer's eyes. Rivera was given an extra fifty years on his twenty-year sentence for the crime. At the time, several police officers were attempting to bring Schaefer up on more charges for further disappearances to make sure he would never get out of prison.

During this time, the tree at C-24 gained a dark reputation. Cloaked figures could be seen at the tree. Stories claimed that a hole in the side of the tree oozed a black sap that could be used for satanic rituals. Some people reported that Schaefer had claimed to hear voices and believed that the tree was somehow secretly in control of the serial killer.

The county eventually purchased the land, created the Oak Hammock Park and began to blaze a path of nature trails through the area. The evil tree was on the list of those to be chopped down. Two loggers were sent in with the task of taking out the old oak. Within minutes of beginning to cut into the tree, their main chainsaw broke. The men, undaunted, brought out their spare. This one malfunctioned as well. Infuriated, the men left for town to buy new equipment. On the way to the hardware store, their car was involved in a serious accident, and both men were killed.

Realizing that they were fighting a losing cause, the county left the tree and diverted the path. It also filled the hole in the tree with cement and hoped that it would die. Instead, the tree grew over the cement, which it wears like a scar. The house near the tree was demolished, and the path was set around the tree.

The tree's legend seems to begin in earnest here. Early versions of the story say that the men were killed due to having bark from the tree in their car. Many believed that taking a piece of the tree and putting it in the vehicle or home of someone you mean to harm would bring about serious misfortune. This legend was fueled by another car accident of a woman who had visited the tree to collect some bark to put in the car of her cheating husband, only to wreck herself with the bark in her passenger seat.

The park is still frequently visited by those trying to take bark and deface the tree. During our visit, there was fresh candlewax on the roots of the tree. Rangers are concerned about all the vandalism of the tree but mostly about someone setting fire to the whole forest. With some new housing in the area, this is a very real concern.

If you do go to Oak Hammock Park, please do so with respect in your hearts for two and possibly more victims of a very sick individual. Offer them some solace and peace and enjoy the beautiful trails along the C-24 Canal and old Florida.

TRAPPER NELSON, HOBE SOUND

What does a shipwrecked Quaker, a top-secret military base and an alligator wrestler have in common? The answer is Jonathan Dickinson State Park in Hobe Sound. This state park comprises more than ten thousand acres. The park includes a variety of natural climates over its expanse. Sand Pine scrublands blend with pine flatwoods, mangroves and river swamps. The Loxahatchee River snakes through a large portion of the park. The river is the first to be designated a National Wild and Scenic River in Florida. The Elsa Kimbell Environmental Education and Research Center is an invaluable resource for information about the park, its ecosystems and its unique history.

The park gets its name from Jonathan Dickinson, a Quaker merchant from the late 1600s. In 1696, he and his family sailed for Philadelphia from Port Royal, Jamaica, on the schooner barque *Reformation*. The ship became separated from its convoy before crashing aground in a hurricane on September 24 near the Jupiter Inlet, which is near present-day Hobe Sound.

The ship suffered no fatalities, but several of the party aboard were injured and ill. The party was soon discovered by the local Jobe Indians. Dickinson misspelled their name in his journals as "Hoe-Bay." After being let loose a few days later to continue their journey, they headed at first for St. Augustine in the small boat salvaged from the *Reformation*. There would be many more trials and tribulations for Jonathan Dickinson and his party before they finally reached Philadelphia in 1697.

Dickinson published his journal of the ordeal in 1699. *Jonathan Dickinson's Journal* is used often as one of the historical "captivity tracts" by educators all over the world. Dickinson also did well in Philadelphia after he arrived. He was twice elected mayor of the city. He died in 1722.

In the early 1900s, Vincent Nostokovich was born to a family of Polish immigrants in Trenton, New Jersey. His parents didn't speak English, so Nelson and his stepbrother, Charles, translated for them. The boys earned money for their family by trapping animals in New Jersey. When their mother died, Vincent and Charles ran away and headed west.

Vince and Charles rode boxcars for a long while. Making money by gambling with other hobos and trapping the occasional animal, the brothers eventually wound up in Mexico. There they were arrested running guns but were freed shortly thereafter. They took to the rails again and eventually made their way to Florida, just north of Jupiter.

Vincent and Charles decided to change their difficult-to-pronounce last name to Nelson. They hunted and trapped animals with a friend and partner they had made named John Dykas, trading their furs in the town of Jupiter. Vince made a name for himself quickly in the town, as he was six-foot-four and weighed about 240 pounds. He used to eat at a local restaurant and was famed for eating a whole pie for lunch. That's right—not just a single piece, a whole pie. One famous account from the diner was of him eating eighteen eggs for breakfast.

In December 1931, Vince's brother, Charles, shot their partner, John, in the back with a shotgun. Vince testified against his stepbrother for the murder. Charles was sentenced to twenty years in prison by Judge C.E. Chillngworth. Charles vowed that when he got out of prison, he would kill the judge and his brother.

Vince retreated into the wilds of Florida and made a camp up the Loxahatchee River far away from the nearby towns but close enough to be able to trade with the locals. He made some decent money during the Great Depression selling furs. He began to purchase the land around his camp as he bid on tax auctions. Sometimes he was bidding against Judge Chillingworth, and the two became friendly rivals in the land market.

Trapper Nelson, as Vince was now being called, began to spruce up his camp with fruit trees and simple huts. When tourists began flocking to the beaches of Florida, some would take notice of Trapper Nelson and his trophies for sale in the local markets. Some would brave the river and boat up to the campsite of this "Wildman of the Loxahatchee."

At first, Trapper would show the folks around for free, but he quickly learned that he could make a few more dollars. He went to work and built Trapper Nelson's Zoo and Jungle Garden. He sold souvenirs and let visitors see the wildlife he kept caged on the grounds. Living the frontier life for so long, without running water or electricity and primarily only eating the animals he killed, Trapper knew that his new guests would like some amenities. He quickly built some cabins and picnic tables and set up some grills.

Tourists flocked to his zoo, and he would show them around for a modest fee. Trapper became a local celebrity and would often swing out over the river to greet the boats bringing fresh guests with a great yell. He earned another nickname as the "Tarzan of the Everglades." Movie stars of the day, most famously Gary Cooper, came to visit his site, and his fame spread. Ladies from the high-brow societies of West Palm Beach often came up to meet the strapping Trapper Nelson, who wrestled alligators.

Between romancing socialites and living the good life in the wilds, Trapper Nelson was doing well for himself. But war was waging in Europe, and America would soon be drawn in. Trapper married a local waitress to attempt to avoid the draft. "Attempt" was the operative word, as he got drafted in 1942, shortly after the wedding. He went to basic training in Texas.

Tearing a leg muscle in training sent him back to Florida. He was posted to the newly erected Camp Murphy, which was right next to where he had his own campsite. He would be serving as an MP at the top-secret base. When he returned to his cabin, he found his new wife cheating on him. A quick divorce occurred while he served at Camp Murphy.

The United States Army Signal Corps established Camp Murphy in 1942. It was the home of the Southern Signal Corps School. It was also the base for instruction in radar operation, a very top-secret technology at the time. At its height, it included more than one thousand buildings and six thousand officers and soldiers. The camp was deactivated in 1944 after less than two years of operation.

Nelson reopened his zoo for the tourists who were starting to return to the area after the war. At this point, he would rent rowboats and overnight cabins. He would wear a loincloth, or his famous swim shorts, and a pith helmet as he would continue to wrestle alligators or handle poisonous snakes for the crowds.

Most of his money went to pay taxes on the nearly one thousand acres he now owned in the area by the mid-1950s. In 1960, health inspectors insisted that he needed to install proper bathrooms at the site. He built them as he had the rest of the camp, but the health inspector insisted that they were not up to code. He forced Nelson to close his zoo. Nelson became a recluse and very distrustful of the government.

Trapper Nelson in front of his chickee cabin at his zoo. *Loxahatchee Historical Society.*

Visitors still came to his camp, but he discouraged it as much as possible. He first posted "No Trespassing" signs. When that didn't work, he put up fences and signs that read, "Danger: Landmines!" Friends would have to let him know ahead of time if they would be visiting. He often carried a twelve-gauge shotgun over his shoulder and would fire it at intruders. Most locals only saw Trapper on his weekly visit to town to pick up mail and restock the local shops with alligator heads and other trinkets.

Trapper could no longer afford the taxes on his land, and he began to look for buyers. He had hoped to sell to some of his former visitors who had money. He had hoped one of them would buy the land and donate it to the state, so it would not be developed like so many of the towns nearby had. He had other trappers in the area with whom he did not get along. Other people wanted his land. Jealous husbands numbered in the dozens. His list of enemies was quite long.

His half brother, Charles, was released from prison around this time. Shortly thereafter, Judge Chillingworth was gunned down. Charles was a suspect but proven innocent, as Chillingworth had been killed by a gunman hired by a rival judge.

In July 1968, Trapper Nelson failed to meet with an old friend. The friend became worried, as Trapper had been in poor health, complaining of frequent stomach pains. When the friend got to the campsite, all appeared well—that is, until he entered Nelson's chickee cabin.

Nelson had been shot in the stomach by his own shotgun. The coroner ruled it a suicide, and the sheriff agreed. Most locals felt that there was foul play. Many felt his brother may have done it. Suicide was possible, but it would have involved him bending over the shotgun to shoot his own stomach. His friends did say that "he would rather die than be an invalid." His recent stomach pains might have been enough to add to his concerns.

Shortly after Trapper's death, the state acquired the land from Nelson's nephew and heir. The site became part of the new Jonathan Dickinson State Park, which already incorporated much of old Camp Murphy next to his property. The site is now Trapper Nelson Zoo Historic District. Although some of the site was damaged by arsonists and vandals before opening to the public, it is now restored and protected by the park.

In 1984, park rangers discovered "Nelson's Treasure" in his chimney while doing restoration work. A cache of 5,005 coins was found that totaled $1,829.46. The coins all dated from the 1890s to the 1960s. No more treasure has been found, even though the site was thoroughly searched.

The camp today is open to the public, but you must get a boat tour from Jonathan Dickinson State Park to visit. You can still visit Trapper's chickee cabin and the remains of his zoo. You can picnic on the Loxahatchee, just like so many have done before you. Keep your eyes open, as the ghost of Trapper Nelson is still said to lurk there, trying to keep trespassers away and woo the ladies.

THE MYSTERY CIRCLE, MIAMI

*I*n the bustling metropolis of Miami, right where the Miami River flows into the Biscayne Bay, there lies a great mystery. Several apartment buildings built in the late 1940s and early 1950s were being torn down to make way for new modern high-rise apartments and condominiums to house Miami's ever-increasing population. The developers purchased the land for millions of dollars, had poured even more money and time into the purchase and were ready to begin the final phase before construction.

In accordance with municipal mandates, an archaeological survey of the site was requested in 1998. As the United States is a relatively young country and only a few hundred years of European settlement history was around, there was not much expected to be found at the site. Even the ancient native inhabitants of the area, mostly Tequesta Indians, were typically hunter/gatherers and thought to be a tribe that continuously migrated.

Digging was a nightmare, as the apartment construction company had poured concrete and built a pool over the site. As these needed to be dug up for the new skyscrapers to be built, the dig was deeper in the ground than usual. What the team found was a strange series of basins dug into the limestone base. The architect of the buildings to be going up recognized the shape as part of an arch and did some quick calculations. He estimated that it was a full circle and asked a digger to cut through the concrete and dirt down to the same level where he estimated the opposite side would be. To his and the archaeologists' surprise, they found matching basins. It was a full circle, nearly thirty-seven feet in diameter.

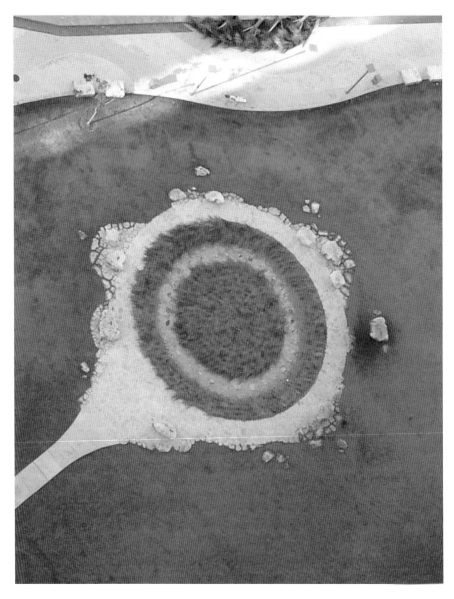

The Miami Mystery Circle from above. *Author's photo.*

Further study began at the site, with theories ranging from it being a point on the Bermuda Triangle to an ancient part of the Olmec or Mayan empires. With such wide-ranging theories, the site became a circus of New Age enthusiasts, native rights groups, historical preservationists and just plain curious sightseers. Cameras were placed on nearby buildings so people could watch the events live on the Internet.

The developer was understandably upset. It had already spent millions to purchase the land. More money had been spent to just get the site to this point. It began to pressure the archaeologists to finish their work. The wild theories seemed to be working against the archaeologists, who knew that they had uncovered a potentially highly culturally significant site. The battle began to save the dig in earnest.

Miami-Dade County finally caved to mounting pressure and purchased the property itself for $27 million. The archaeologists could begin their work anew. At this point, they were able to bring in fresh experts. One expert, while reviewing photos of the site, realized that there was a septic tank right on one of the basins. Could this circle just be runoff for the old apartment buildings? Had Miami just paid $27 million for a sewage system? A quick check of plans of the old buildings proved that the system fed into a sewer and had no runoff. A bullet had been dodged, but still no answers on the purpose of the circle could be found.

Further excavation found numerous holes in seemingly random locations dug into the limestone. Strange artifacts began to be uncovered, including two perfect basalt axe heads, teeth from an extinct species of seal and a shell carapace of a sea turtle not native to the area. These odd items were researched thoroughly, and the axe heads were found to match those of natives of northern Georgia more than six hundred miles away. These finds led the team to realize that this must have been quite a trade hub from the ancient people.

Suddenly, a picture was beginning to form, a realization that the Tequesta Indians must have been much more advanced than originally thought. A carving of an eye and fragments of unique metals and alignment of the basins seemed to point to ritualistic purposes for the site. Still, the hundreds of strange postholes they had uncovered just seemed to bring up more questions than answers.

If the site was a ritual site, then why was there no sign of a central hearth, as is common with most such sites? There were no signs of any burning at what was now called the "Miami Mystery Circle." The Tequesta Indians had used stingray tail barbs, alligator teeth and shark teeth to make remarkably efficient drills for digging the post holes into the limestone. Geologists were called in to try to date the holes, and they dated the crust that had grown around them to be thousands of years old. This put the site as the oldest significant historical human construction on the eastern side of the United States.

Finally, they realized why they had never found signs of a hearth or fire. The Tequestas had built the site on stilts to avoid the frequent storms and summer flooding rains so common in tropical Florida. Archaeologists also theorized that the randomness of the holes was simply them shoring up old holes as the humidity and rain rotted out the old wood. This would mean that the buildings at the site had stayed in one location for hundreds of years. This revelation totally shattered the image of the nomadic Tequestas and showed them to be a truly remarkable civilization.

An image began to appear of a settlement with a large structure built for ceremonial purposes—a large conical building of wood with a raised floor and open roof. Small buildings around the central site would have provided limited housing. A cultural center for the Tequestas had never even been thought of, but here it was. Sadly, the tribe had died shortly after European settlement of Florida between wars and disease. No single person identifies as a member of the lost Tequesta tribe to this day.

In 2003, Senator Bob Graham helped pass legislation that authorized the site being added to Biscayne National Park. The dig continued for years, but every storm season put it at further risk. It was decided to rebury the site to continue to preserve it.

The Miami Circle now rests in the middle of a waterfront park. Signs and an audio tour are available for visitors to this wonderful hideaway in the shadows of high-rise apartments and condos. Boats still pass through Biscayne Bay and into the Miami River, right next to this ancient site that may have had boats come through before even the Parthenon was completed.

Archaeologists continue to study the Tequesta Indians and their site here in the hopes of discovering even more about the earliest inhabitants of what is now Miami.

THE ISLE OF BONES AND THE CORPSE BRIDE
OF THE CONCH REPUBLIC, KEY WEST

*I*n 1513, when Spanish explorer Ponce de Leon arrived in what would become Florida, he came upon an island covered with bones stacked on bones. These were the remains of battles and the ancient burial ground for the Calusa Indians. The sheer size and scope of the number of bodies gave Ponce de Leon cause for concern. However, it was the westernmost key with a reliable supply of water and was less than one hundred miles from the Spanish colony in Cuba. He called the island Casa Hueso, the Isle of Bones. Many years later, it would become Key West.

The island became host to a Spanish fishing village. It wasn't long before a steady stream of salvage operators began operating in the area to retrieve goods from the numerous shipwrecks nearby. The Spanish left a small garrison there to help maintain order in the small island colony. It was nearly the halfway mark from Havana to Miami, and the Spanish used the deepwater port there for resupply quite often.

Key West and much of the rest of the Florida Keys are on the dividing line between the Atlantic Ocean and the Gulf of Mexico. The two large bordering seas have different currents. The Gulf of Mexico has warmer and calmer seas; the Atlantic contains much wilder seas. The Straits of Florida is the name of the area where these two bodies of water merge into one between Key West and Cuba. This area became strategically and economically important for everyone in Florida.

Great Britain took control of Florida in 1762. The Spanish and most of the Native American population of Key West left for Havana. Many were forcibly removed from the Casa Hueso. The British did little to the island and sent few settlers to it. The garrison of soldiers there was simply there in support of the British Royal Navy as it operated in the Straits of Florida.

When the Spanish regained Florida twenty years later, after the American Revolutionary War, few Spanish citizens returned to Florida. Fewer still returned to Casa Hueso. The island remained a community of British and Cuban fishermen and some new settlers from the fledgling United States. The island, though claimed by Spain, still acted mostly independently.

The Spanish governor of Cuba decided in 1815 to deed the entire island of Casa Hueso to a Royal Spanish Navy officer from St. Augustine named Juan Pablo Salas. Before he was able to do much of anything with the island, Spain lost Florida in the Adams-Onis Treaty in 1821. Juan Pablo Salas sold the island for a sloop valued under $600 to General John Geddes, a retired governor of South Carolina. A businessman named John W. Simonton approached Salas with an offer for the island a short while later, and at a café in Havana, the deal was struck: the Spaniard sold the island again for about $2,000 in pesos.

The resulting dispute of the two owners of the island would have a long and tumultuous legal battle that played out in faraway Washington. Simonton and a friend of his named John Whitehead fought with Geddes for clear title to the island. Whitehead had been shipwrecked and stranded in Key West in 1819 and knew of the potential of the "Gibraltar of the West." Using political clout, Simonton and Whitehead gained control of the island.

In March 1822, the United States flag was planted on the island for the first time. No one in Key West seemed to care, and so the Florida Keys became part of the United States. Shortly thereafter, the island came under the direct rule of Commodore David Porter. Porter was in command of the United States Navy West Indies Anti-Pirate Squadron. He instated martial law on the island. Many did not appreciate the blockades and soldiers stifling trade. Commodore Porter saw it as necessary to end piracy and illegal trade, including slave ships, around the Straits of Florida. This only lasted a short time, as Porter was reassigned, and the island began to thrive.

By 1830, Key West had become the richest city per capita in America. Wealthy investors flocked to the island to open numerous business ventures. The biggest money came from the salt industry. At low tide, the commodity was harvested from the sea instead of from mines as elsewhere. Immigrants from the Bahamas and Cuba came by the boatloads. Many were able to make a very good living between fishing, turtling, salvaging and salt harvesting.

The Bahamian immigrants who were arriving in ever-increasing numbers throughout the mid-1800s were known as "Conchs," named after the conch seashells they would often retrieve while harvesting salt or fishing. A custom from the time that remains in Key West is that when a baby was born to one of these people, they would put a conch shell on a pole in front of the house. The name has stuck for hundreds of years now for residents of Key West.

Construction of Fort Zachary Taylor on the island came in 1845 from the same program that led to Fort Pickens in Pensacola and many other sea forts after the War of 1812. Two supporting batteries were built "cannon distance" apart. These are the Martello Towers, which helped increase the coverage of the shipping lanes and defend the port of Key West.

At the outset of the Civil War, the fort came under the command of Union captain John Brannon, who moved his forty-four men into Fort Zachary Taylor. He defended the fort from Confederate forces. It was then used as a key outpost to stop Confederate blockade runners attempting to ship supplies through the Straits of Florida.

After the end of the Civil War, Cuban refugees began to flood the island. They brought with them a cigar industry that would later move to Tampa, but for a long while, it flourished in Key West, with tobacco being imported directly from Cuba. One day, a large fire that started at a cigar club engulfed the town. In all, 18 cigar factories and 614 other buildings were destroyed, including most of the government buildings. The town rebounded once again. By 1889, the city was booming, once more becoming the richest per capita city in America.

The USS *Maine* sailed from Key West in January 1898 to protect U.S. interests during the Cuban War of Independence. Less than three weeks later, a large explosion on board the *Maine* sank the boat in Havana Harbor. With most of the crew asleep or in their quarters, many lost their lives as 260 men died. The cause of the explosion was declared a Spanish mine in the harbor, but it is still uncertain what actually happened. Though not a direct cause of the Spanish-American War, the rallying cry, "Remember the *Maine*! To hell with Spain!" echoed throughout the United States. Within two months of the sinking, we were at war.

Key West boomed again with so much naval support in the town. Many of the crew of the *Maine* were buried in Key West at the early beginnings of the large Key West Cemetery. The town supported the war effort as much as possible. The war ended after a few months, and life returned once again to normal in the Florida Keys.

World wars and a particularly disastrous hurricane in 1935 both helped and hindered the Keys. The Labor Day Hurricane of 1935 destroyed the Overseas Railroad that Henry Flagler had built to connect the Keys to the Florida mainland in 1912. Using the remnants of "Flagler's Folly," though, allowed for the extension of the Overseas Highway, and U.S. Route 1 was completed to Key West by 1938. World Wars I and II both brought more navy support to the town but also made shipping and trade more difficult.

During the Great Depression, a man named Carl Tanzler emigrated from Germany, leaving his wife and two young daughters behind in his home country. He tried to find work in Austria, but after a few years, he headed for Cuba. When he still found no living wage, he came to Zephyrhills to meet his sister, who had traveled there years earlier. He sent for his wife and daughters. Still finding work hard to come by locally, he read of the booming city of Key West far to the south.

Leaving his wife and children again, he decided to reinvent himself in his new home. He started calling himself Count Carl Tanzler von Cosel. He claimed that he was of German royalty and had nine degrees from various universities. He was now an electrical inventor and doctor. He had also been a submarine captain. Using this new identity, he procured a job as a pathologist and X-ray technician at the U.S. Marine Hospital in Key West just outside Fort Zachary Taylor.

While growing up in Germany, Carl had claimed to have been visited by the ghost of one of his ancestors, Countess Constantina von Cosel. She would visit him frequently and give him visions of his future. One vision was the face of his true love, an exotic dark-haired woman. He was obsessed with finding her his whole life.

In 1926, Elena Milagro de Hoyos was pregnant with the child of her husband, Luis Mesa. The Cuban immigrant couple had just moved to Key West, with Luis working in a large cigar factory. When she miscarried, Luis left her. Tragedy after tragedy seemed to follow Elena—members of her family had become ill with tuberculosis—and she soon felt cursed.

On April 22, 1930, Carl was working at the Marine Hospital when Elena came in, as she had also gotten the dreaded TB. Tanzler was convinced that Elena was the woman in his visions. He insisted on treating her and tried everything he could to save her life. He also began buying her presents of jewelry and fancy clothing. He professed his love for her. She was twenty-two years old and Tanzler was fifty-five. Elena was flattered but merely wanted to get better.

The courtship was not to last, as Tanzler was unable to help her, perhaps because he was not a real doctor and TB was even deadlier at that time than it is today. Elena died and was buried in a plain grave. Tanzler asked the Hoyos family if he could build her an aboveground tomb for his beloved Elena that he would pay for. The family did not object, and she was moved to the tomb. What the family did not know was that Carl had a key to the tomb.

Every night, Tanzler would visit Elena. He would bring her flowers and gifts. He would also let himself in and sleep beside her corpse. At one point, he installed a telephone in the crypt to speak to Elena from beyond the grave. He was convinced that she spoke to him through such electronic devices.

This ritual went on for several months, and then Tanzler took Elena back to a wingless fuselage of an airplane behind the Marine Hospital. Her body had already decomposed quite a bit. Tanzler rebuilt her body by working piano wire through the bones. He stuffed her body with rags. He gave her a pair of glass eyes and replaced her skin with layers of silk soaked in wax. He even made a wig for her from hairs he had received from Elena's mother after the funeral.

Tanzler bought her fancy clothes and other finery. He was often seen in town buying perfumes in large quantities. He used this to hide her increasing stench. He also went so far as to insert a tube into her body so they could have marital relations. His madness seemed to know no bounds.

The Marine Hospital eventually tired of Carl and fired him. He also learned that his wingless plane was going to soon be scrapped. He took Elena's body to his home. There he placed her on his bed and continued to rub her body with chemicals and oils. He decided that he would need to build an airship to fly into the stratosphere where the radiation of the sun could help revive his true love. Her ghost had apparently told him that she couldn't wait to return to him.

Elena's sister heard tales of Carl in town buying perfumes and dresses. She even heard the story of a young paperboy who saw "the Count dancing with a large Frankenstein Doll." She notified the authorities, who searched the mausoleum and found it empty. She went to Tanzler's house to confront him.

The count welcomed his "sister-in-law" into his home. She saw what she originally thought was a wax dummy in the likeness of Elena dressed in a wedding gown lying on the bed. The overpowering smell of flowers and perfumes was not quite enough to hide the scent of decay. Carl told her that they were very happy together and that she should come and visit them for dinner some night. Elena's sister went immediately back to the police.

Count Carl Tanzler von Cosel with Dr. DePoo and attorney Louis Harris. *From the DeWolfe and Wood Collection in the Otto Hirzel Scrapbook, Key West Historical Society.*

Carl was arrested for mistreatment of a corpse and grave robbery. By the time the case went to trial, however, the statute of limitations on the grave robbing charge had expired, since he had been living with Elena for nine years. The crime could only be prosecuted for seven years. As the trial went on for the other charge, a large number of women visited the courtroom in support of Tanzler. Many felt that it was romantic of the old man to dedicate his life to try to bring back his lost love. If only the papers had reported the more lurid details of Carl's "undying love," particularly the acts of necrophilia, Carl's fan club probably would not have been so sympathetic to the old man.

The judge finally had enough when Tanzler, still calling himself Count Von Cosel, asked for Elena's body back. He still intended to build an airship to take Elena to the skies to restore her to life. He was sent to psychiatrists for evaluation. They said that he was sane and let him go. Carl was a free man.

Elena had received so much publicity that the local funeral home placed her corpse on display for tourists. One description of the sight is as follows: "I've never been able to forget that sight. It didn't even look like a human

The death mask of Elena Milagro de Hoyos. *Author's photo.*

anymore. So much reconstruction and decay…it was the scariest thing I'd ever seen. Her face was an odd white-ish color that looked more like a wax dummy than a woman's face. And she had horrible black, staring, glass eyes. I still dream about that sight."

Elena was reburied a short while later in an undisclosed location. Tanzler had become an odd celebrity and wrote an autobiography. He would give tours of his home and lab to tourists fascinated by the macabre story of the mysterious count and his corpse bride. He also went on to write numerous stories for *Fantastic Adventures* and other pulp magazines of the era. Most of his stories involved love from beyond the grave.

In 1952, Carl was found dead in his home after having not been seen for several weeks. He was found lying on another dummy he had made of Elena, with another death mask he had copied from the original one he had made for his beloved lost love. He had returned to his wife and daughters, who still lived in Zephyrhills. Although he still had the mask and dummy body, they apparently knew nothing of the madness of Carl Tanzler.

Key West continues to be no stranger to madness. In 1982, a blockade was set up on U.S. 1, where the Overseas Highway meets the mainland United States at Florida City. The intent was to search for illegal immigrants from the Mariel Boatlift, a large emigration of Cubans fleeing a massive decline in the Cuban economy. Castro had stated in 1980 that anyone wishing to leave Cuba could do so out of the port of Mariel as long as someone came to pick them up in a boat.

Cuban exiles in the United States flooded Miami and Key West and rented boats by the thousands to go and try to free relatives from the communist country to the south. Initially, public support for this was widespread. This changed quickly when quite a few of the refugees were found to be released criminals and mental patients from Cuba's overcrowded and understaffed facilities. Although the majority of refugees were ordinary Cubans, public sentiment quickly changed.

The blockade at Florida City caused a seventeen-mile traffic jam as the border patrol checked every car leaving the Keys for illegal immigrants. This effectively paralyzed the Florida Keys and its lifeblood of tourism. When the city's complaints went unanswered by the U.S. federal government, Mayor Dennis Wardlow and the Key West City Council declared their independence and seceded from the United States.

According to the city council, the U.S. government had set up a border station as though the Florida Keys composed a separate nation. It decided to become one. Since many local citizens still called themselves Conchs, they became the Conch Republic. Mayor Wardlow became Prime Minister Wardlow of the Conch Republic. He immediately declared war on the United States. One minute later, he announced that seeing as their cause was hopeless, the Conch Republic surrendered to the United States. However, it did immediately ask for $1 billion in foreign aid.

The secession was a huge success in drawing attention to the plight of the Keys, and the roadblocks were quickly removed. The fame also created another boom of tourists, and Conch Republic flags and memorabilia are still sold today.

Several other incidents occurred over the years that brought back the Conch Republic. On September 20, 1995, the 478th Civil Affairs Battalion of the United States Army Reserve began an unusual training operation. The battalion was to land on Key West and act as though the islands were a foreign nation. The problem was that no one from the 478th told anyone in Key West about the operation.

When the community first got news of the training exercise, word spread through the small island community like wildfire. Seizing this chance for publicity, the organizers of the 1982 secession reformed the Conch Republic and mobilized their nation for war. Former prime minister Wardlow was brought out of retirement, and he organized the island forces for defense. For his ground troops, this consisted of arming the locals with stale Cuban bread loaves to hit soldiers with. For his naval forces, he had the fireboats of the island fire their water cannons at the "hostile invaders."

The leadership of the 478th issued an apology the next day, noting that they "in no way meant to challenge or impugn the sovereignty of the Conch Republic." They submitted to formal surrender to Wardlow in a ceremony on September 22. In this ceremony, Wardlow hit the commanding officer on the head with a stale loaf of Cuban bread.

In Key West today, you can visit Fort Zachary Taylor National Park and watch out the windows where they once defended the port from pirates and marauders. You can also visit Fort East Martello, which is now the Fort East Martello Museum. The museum is most famous for "Robert the Doll," who we covered in *Eerie Florida*. However, the museum also has a new exhibit. It has parts of Elena de Hoyos's original mausoleum, which Tanzler had blown up at one point. It also has the death mask and dummy that Tanzler lived with after Elena had been reburied.

With so many ghost tours, dark history and legends in Key West, it is easy to see why so many still call it Casa Hueso, the Isle of Bones.

IN CLOSING

Once again, dear reader, we find ourselves at the end of our latest collection of odd places, myths, monsters and legends. We hope you enjoyed the tales and maybe even learned a little history about this crazy state of ours. We've hit more dirt roads, highways and places off the beaten path between the two books than I thought even existed. I still think we've only just scratched the surface.

Again, we followed trails blazed by our peers. Tellers of tall tales, ghost story experts, cryptozoologists, historians and more have traveled these paths long before we did. Thankfully, we found a few stones they hadn't completely uncovered along the way.

We've been traveling the convention circuit heavily in between our expeditions. We're really racking up hotel reward points. We've met numerous new friends. We've grown reacquainted with old ones. We've also got even more stories to tell.

If you enjoyed this book, find us online at EerieFlorida.com. There you'll be able to see color photos, videos and other legends that we couldn't squeeze into the two books. We also have some of our radio and podcast appearances linked. With those, you can get some audio versions of the stories as well.

So, now the question is: will there be a third book? Well, that is up to you all. Go out and convince your friends to buy our books. Have them get their friends to buy our books. Once The History Press sees there's still demand, I'm sure it will ask us back for a third time. There's plenty more stories to tell.

Until then, keep the ghost light burning. We'll see you on the other side.

The author, illustrator and a door to adventure. *Author's photo.*

ABOUT THE AUTHOR AND THE ILLUSTRATOR

MARK MUNCY is the creator of Hellview Cemetery, a charity haunted house in Central Florida that was so infamous it was banned by the City of St. Petersburg. An author of horror and science fiction, he has spent more than three decades collecting ghostly tales and reports of legendary beasts. This is his second book for The History Press after the successful *Eerie Florida* in 2017. He lives in St. Petersburg, Florida, on the remains of an ancient midden with his fiancée, Kari Schultz. Occasionally, he is visited by his daughters when they remember he is still there.

KARI SCHULTZ is a varied illustrator at Fox Dream Studio who enjoys fantasy and horror. She has been working on art as long as she can remember and reading folklore and horror almost as long. She has a short comic featured in *Uncanny Adventures: Duo #2* from 8th Wonder Press. This is her second work for The History Press. She has a thing for foxes. She occasionally ventures out of her dwelling in St. Petersburg in search of cryptids. She can also at times be lured forth with ice cream.

Visit us at
www.historypress.com